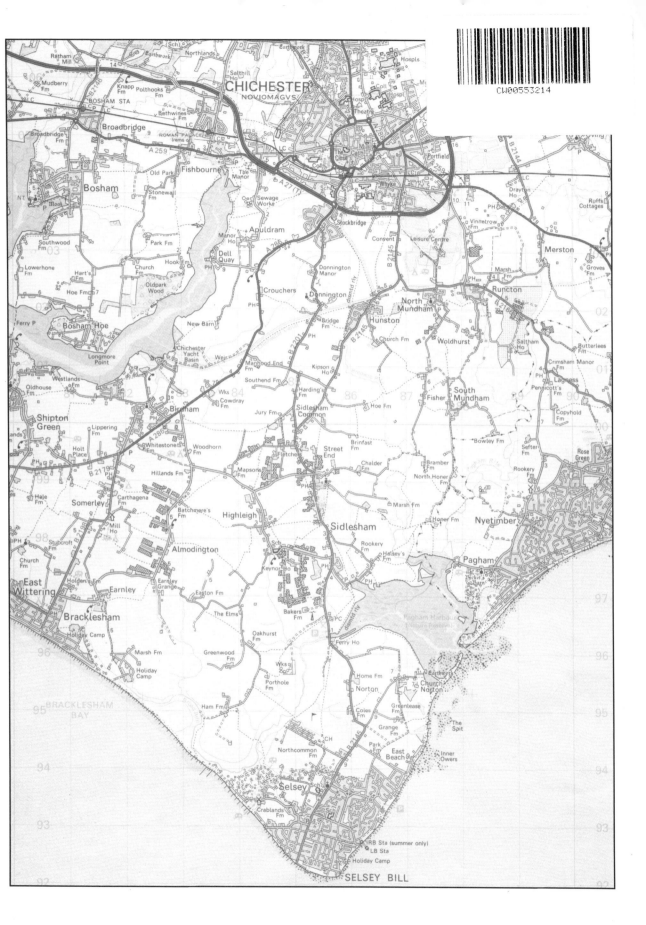

THE SELSEY TRAM

NOTICE IS HEREBY GIVEN

That, owing to the flooding of the line between Sidlesham and Ferry, all Cheap Bookings are suspended. Also the Company cannot Book Passengers through from Chichester to Selsey, or vice versa. Arrangements have been made, however, to run a 'Bus Service between Mill Pond Halt and Ferry. Every reasonable effort will be made by the Company to maintain this Service, but it cannot be guaranteed, and the Company will not be responsible for same.

Through Passengers must book locally on each section of the line, viz., Chichester and Mill Pond Halt, and Ferry and Selsey.

Selsey, December, 1910.   H. G. PHILLIPS, Manager.

Flood warning, 1910.

THE SELSEY TRAM

David Bathurst

Phillimore

1992

Published by
PHILLIMORE & CO. LTD.,
Shopwyke Hall, Chichester, Sussex

ISBN 0 85033 839 5

Printed and bound in Great Britain by
BIDDLES LTD.,
Guildford, Surrey

Contents

List of Illustrations

Frontispiece Flood warning, 1910

Acknowledgements

There are a very large number of people to whom I owe a considerable debt of thanks in preparing this book. A full bibliography is contained at the end of the book. However, special thanks in preparing the text are due to the West Sussex County Records Office for allowing me access to so much important documentation; to *Railway Magazine* for providing the articles by Buckell, Whitechurch and Nicol, (and to David & Charles, publishers, for allowing me to quote from John Scott-Morgan's splendid book on the Colonel Stephens Railway). I have also received invaluable material from local residents in response to requests for information most notably Winifred Langer, Vernon Fogden, Henrietta Conduit, Brian Langmead, Peter Ogden (who provided some important Selsey Parish Council material), Dick Allen and above all Mr. E. Green, whose material was so sparkling and informative that it has been allocated an appendix all to itself.

Finally, I must acknowledge the enormous contributions made by Jeff Vinter, Chairman of the Railway Ramblers, who encouraged me every step of the way and who provided a number of contact points; Noel Osborne, Editorial Director of Phillimore, who has provided the incentive for me to complete the work; my thanks to Peter Fuller of Ashley Courtenay for his support and my wife Lizzie who, ably assisted by Jill Thorne, deciphered my appalling handwriting to put this book into a state acceptable to my publisher.

David Bathurst

Picture Acknowledgements

I have had to lean very heavily on the goodwill and generosity of others for illustrative material, and a huge debt of thanks is owed to: R. M. Casserley, 9, 40, 48, 60-1; Chichester District Museum, 2, 4-5, 8, 13, 18-20, 23, 34, 49, 56; A. Coffin, 12, 47, 52, 55; J. Fisher, 74-5; N. Hermon-Taylor, 72; A. Hill, 1, 10, 15, 22, 26, 33, 68-9; National Railway Museum, York, 14, 32, 41, 57; Peter Richards, the 1934 report and 7, 24-5, 43-6, 63, 76-7, 80; West Sussex County Record Office, 59; J. Wynne-Tyson, 6, 11, 17, 42, 50-1, 78-9, 86-9, 97. Thanks also to the Ordnance Survey for permission to reproduce the maps used in the book.

Introduction

One of the saddest aspects of progress is the discarding of services, amenities and facilities that are no longer considered relevant, however useful or essential they may once have been. In the latter half of the 20th century, this has been witnessed on an unprecedented scale. The local shop, which has maintained a faithful and dependent clientèle, gives way to the out of town superstore. The 'manager' of any business is no more to be found in an upstairs office but in a gargantuan soulless redbrick complex 80 miles away. Typed, personal letters are replaced by computerised slips prepared by a wordprocessor.

In no aspect of 20th-century life, though, has this trend been more pronounced than in the field of transport. The steady decline of the beloved country railway at the hands of massive expansion of road travel is almost a cliché, and more than amply documented elsewhere. Yet there can be few more striking examples of the personal, 'user friendly' country railway lines than the subject of this book, the Chichester to Selsey Railway line, better known as the Selsey Tramway. Few railways, however rural or antiquated, can boast trains which waited at stations for tardy passengers; which engaged in races with cyclists; whose customers included a mouse-trap salesman; whose rolling stock did daily battle with cows straying on to the line; and whose services had to be suspended owing to a temperamental drawbridge. The end, when it finally came, closed the curtain on this extraordinary affair, and heralded the era we now know, the impersonal rumble of rubber on well-worn tarmacadam.

Surprisingly little has been written about the line, and it was a sense of intrigue about its quaintness and uniqueness, and the factors which led to its becoming discarded, that inspired the writing of this book.

Having decided on the subject matter, the main concern has been to set objectives and to decide at which readership to aim. With the greatest respect to their esteemed and learned authors, the bookshelves are saturated with highly technical railway histories, of great interest to the railway buff but of little interest to the general reader or local historian. Certainly it is to be hoped that this book will provide the railway buff with all the essential detail he needs. However, it is also to be hoped that the reader will find here more than just a bald railway history. The 'historical' chapters are liberally laced with stories, press-cuttings and anecdotes which will be of interest to the social and local historian too; this is especially true of the chapters devoted to humour and happenings on the line. The last part of the book, however, takes the line out of the realms of history and plants it firmly into the modern age; there is a chapter devoted to modern-day reminders of the line's existence, and another chapter written especially for those who wish to walk the line themselves, and from that to progress to exploration of other lines. No apology is made for assuming the status of guide book in this chapter.

In summary, this book aims to do three things: firstly, to provide an entertaining, informative and vigorous account of the line between the first tentative proposals in the 1880s, and the administration of the last rites some 50 years later; secondly, to remind the reader that a line's history does not end with the last train – that it is a continuing story with a part still to play in local life, helping to mitigate the 'discarding' process already alluded to; and thirdly to inspire the more athletic not only to explore the beautiful countryside through which the line passed, but also to seek out the disused railways in their own locality and so cultivate a fascinating and worthwhile hobby.

The historical chapters have, as far as possible, dealt with the line's main events in chronological order. In certain chapters, though, particularly those devoted to Tramway happenings and humour, a certain amount of 'jumping about' is not only necessary but desirable. To describe the line's events in a clinical, chronological fashion is to be insensitive to the significance of the events and the readability of the history as a whole. Certain stories and events could just as easily fit in one chapter as another; some sort of overlap is inevitable, but it is to be hoped that repetition has been kept to a minimum.

A wide readership has been targeted in the preparation of this book: railway and local historians, walkers and specifically railway ramblers. In doing so, there is the inherent risk of pleasing one group at the expense of boring the others, yet this book will have succeeded if any reader feels he or she has been enriched in his or her pursuit of one of the above activities by a perusal of what follows, and in being enriched has been entertained.

Chapter One

Origins and Opening

The village of Selsey lies eight miles to the south of Chichester, and represents the southernmost community in Sussex. Together with the parishes of Bracklesham, the Witterings, Itchenor, Birdham, Donnington, Apuldram, Hunston and Sidlesham, it forms the Manhood Peninsula, which on a map of West Sussex appears to be something of an afterthought; a little piece tacked on to a county whose downlands for the most part hug the succession of coastal settlements starting with Bognor and finishing at Hove. Unlike most of Sussex, then, where a wide variety of towns and villages await the traveller in a 10-mile radius, the traveller starting from Selsey has little choice but to venture north, only at Chichester reaching the point where he can choose to head for the downland of rural Sussex or the urban sprawl in southeast Hampshire.

A good system of communication between Selsey and Chichester has always been a necessity, and as the turn of the last century approached, railwaymen and non-railwaymen alike began to see how this could be achieved by means of rail transport. Not only would it serve Selsey folk wishing to reach out to the rest of civilisation, but it would also be a means of providing access to the seaside for the people of Chichester and its environs.

Although Selsey nowadays is overshadowed by Chichester in terms of historical interest and by nearby Bognor Regis for the sun-and-fun lover, there were a number of people who saw in the village a certain charm. It was described before the line opened as 'a pretty and unconventional resort, in great favour with the legal fraternity, and with people who reside there during the season, paterfamilias dividing his time between London and Selsey'. Another commentator described Selsey as 'an interesting and picturesque village'. Whitechurch called it 'the resort of those who like quiet and retirement by the shore, pure air and a glorious view of the Isle of Wight'. A Ward Lock guide was more frank: 'No-one who knows the district would travel thither for the scenery, but it makes a very restful and pleasant holiday resort away from the beaten track'. Magan, in an article in *Sussex County Magazine*, recalled how, in the middle of the 19th century, although the 'ancient city of Selsey' had been reduced to a fishing village, 'new life was stirring' and going to the seaside was 'becoming a right to even larger numbers of city dwellers: a legacy of gentle, cosy things'. He said that the 'growing holiday potential and absence of physical obstacles promised well'.

It was clear, therefore, that with more money in the pockets of the city dwellers, and the expansion of the main rail network right across Sussex, there was potential for villages like Selsey to expand into bustling resorts, if only the passengers could be transported there. At the same time, there was clearly a need for a more effective system of transport from Selsey to Chichester: a Mrs. Terry, talking of her childhood in Hunston, recalls the days of the horsedrawn carriers, and in particular a Mrs. Burtenshaw of Sidlesham: 'If you wanted her to do any shopping for you', she said, 'you had to put a clothes prop up in the hedge with a duster tied on, and she used to come down and see what you wanted'. One local carrier, indeed the only carrier in the 1870s, was Mr. Fidler, and his journey to Chichester took two hours from Selsey: the return trip could take even longer if the driver took advantage of the public houses en route. The only alternative if one did not own a horse was to walk.

The most obvious means of achieving better communications between Chichester and Selsey was by rail. The rail network was expanding all the time, and had come to Chichester in 1846. The ground between Chichester and Selsey was almost completely flat, posing no great construction difficulties. Following the arrival of the main line it was inevitable that it would not be long before the idea of a rail link to Selsey was seriously mooted, and in 1887 Messrs. Frederick Grafton and Charles Cranford got together and drew up an application to Parliament for an Act to 'incorporate a company and empower it to make and maintain a railway seven miles, seven furlongs and two chains long from Chichester, commencing at a junction with the main line, and terminating near the coastguard station at Selsey; and landing stage one hundred yards long, seven chains north-east of Beacon House'. Plans were duly deposited for what was proposed to be the Selsey Railway and Pier Act 1888.

Perhaps deterred by the estimated cost – £75,000 – the project never proceeded, and for seven years plans to link the main network with Selsey hung in abeyance. Then in 1895 came a significant event, the Light Railways Bill. This was the most positive step yet taken by Parliament in the field of railway construction. Up until that time no railway or tramway could be constructed unless a special act of Parliament was obtained. Light Railways, under the Act, would now be able to be constructed without any application to Parliament, simply by obtaining the consent of the Transport Commissioners. This would obviously make it far cheaper and easier to build and run a Light Railway.

Buckell, in his *Light Railways*, was most enthusiastic about this, pointing out that light railways could facilitate the transportation of agricultural produce to the main lines so farmers could put produce into the markets more easily, thus providing a good remedy for agricultural depression. As far as Selsey and its environs were concerned, this was a particularly pertinent consideration. The area round Selsey was heavily farmed: it must be remembered that Pagham Harbour had been reclaimed by the land and was an area greatly valued for agricultural purposes. A railway between this coastal area and Chichester would be immensely beneficial to the local economy. The Selsey Parish Council was quick to see this, and when in 1895 Mr. E. V. Ivatts, who had been the real inspiration behind the 1888 plan, initiated a simpler scheme for a railway between Chichester and Selsey but without a pier, they made an enthusiastic proposal at their meeting of 7 May. It stated:

> that a committee consisting of five members should be appointed to help forward in any way practicable the present scheme for building a light railway from Chichester to Selsey and to watch the progress of the Light Railway Bill now before the House of Commons and, should it receive Royal Assent, to secure at Selsey at the earliest possible date, the advantages it may provide, and take advantage of any other opportunity that may present itself of carrying out the object in view.

1. The *Chichester* being hauled along the road during construction of the line, in 1897, with the aid of rails that were set down and then lifted as the locomotive passed over them. The father of Mr. Hill, who provided this photo, remembers the *Chichester* being brought through Eastgate Square, Chichester, and coming off the rails in doing so.

Doubtless the members had in mind not just the agriculturalists but local residents and visitors.

The Light Railways Act duly became law. A survey was made by Messrs. Powell & Co. of Lewes with a view to assessing the feasibility of a line between Chichester and Selsey. On 23 March 1896 an inaugural public meeting was held, led by Messrs. James, Newton and Clayton, the promoters of the new project, and it was decided to press ahead with a plan to construct a railway, without a pier. The original plan had been to run it east of the Chichester canal, although this later changed for reasons that will become apparent. A company whose objects were to build and manage the railway was incorporated and registered as a limited liability company on 29 April 1896. Authority was given in the Memorandum of Association to apply for, promote and obtain any Act of Parliament, provisional order or licence of the Board of Trade or other authority for the company to carry any of its objects into effect. The final decision to proceed was taken on 15 January 1897, the contract for its construction going to Mancktelow Brothers. The first directors are recorded as G. Woodbridge J.P., J. Clayton, R. Thornton, J. Framfield, Alderman W. Smith J.P., R. H. Powell, Alderman Sharp Garland J.P., H. J. Powell and L. Clayton. The engineer was to be

Holman Stephens, who had associations with Powell & Co., had formulated plans at a preliminary meeting, and had been involved in the construction of other similar railways. His story is told more fully in the next chapter. It was recorded, prophetically as it turned out, that 'it is not intended or desired to run trains at an express speed'.

With the exception of Stephens, all those who subscribed to the company following incorporation were Sussex residents, making it a truly local project fuelled by local interest: the names Sharp Garland and Clayton, for example, have enjoyed a long association with the Chichester and Selsey area. It was therefore not altogether surprising that the directors found that, by making some amendments to the proposed route, leading the *Chichester Observer* to refer to the line's 'tortuous and winding character', it was possible to purchase all the land by private arrangement, based largely on personal contacts and influences, without the need to worry about obtaining compulsory purchase orders. Hence the reference by Mr. Heron-Allen, for many years chairman of the tramway company, to its 'hugging the hedges in an apparently needless manner'. It was also decided that, in view of the nature of the operation, particularly its avowed intention not to run trains at an excess speed, there was in fact no need to obtain a Light Railway Order under the new legislation. The railway, instead of being known as such, would be known as a 'tramway', ostensibly complying with the legislation appropriate to the running of trams. Hence the name of the company was 'The Hundred of Manhood and Selsey Tramway Company', and the name by which the line was always known – the Selsey Tram – even though it was not a tram at all. The authority contained in the Memorandum of Association was never in fact required.

The great advantage to the company of the arrangement was that it exempted them from Board of Trade scrutiny and it enabled them to construct the permanent way very cheaply, because at the numerous road crossings there was no obligation to provide safety measures expected of even the lightest of Light Railways. It was only when the company began to contemplate the possible adoption of the route by Southern Railway after the Great War that serious measures were taken to legalise the railway as a railway. That did not stop Ward Lock in 1919 calling it 'the Chichester and Selsey Light Railway'.

Work on the permanent way began in May 1897, and by August of that year construction was complete – apart from Chichester terminus station, not ready on opening – as far as the point in Selsey at which the road was to cross over the line by means of a bridge. The bridge was yet to be completed, as was Selsey Town station 200 yards further on, and the Selsey Beach extension, which was not in fact completed for another year.

And so it was that on 27 August 1897, crowds assembled at Chichester station for the inauguration of the Selsey tramway.

Opening
Although the line's headquarters was to be situated in Selsey, the line's opening, presumably because of the incomplete state of the main station there, was to take place at Chichester. So it was that one o'clock on that late August day found an expectant

2.   The enthusiastic gathering at Chichester for the tramway's opening, on 27 August 1897. The platform at Chichester was later extended, and a water tank built.

crowd of official guests, including the mayor and mayoress, Alderman and Mrs. Ballard, directors and shareholders, waiting on the little platform at Chichester for the arrival of the first train, which was in turn to convey the guests to Selsey for lunch.

The train, headed by a locomotive named *Chichester*, had to start from Selsey, and actually conveyed to Chichester a number of Selsey residents who were to take part in the ceremony. It may have been this latter factor which contributed to a delay of nearly an hour, the dignitaries cooling their heels on the platform; as the *Chichester Observer* put it, 'their patience must have been nearly exhausted when at last it was seen slowly coming round the bend'. The *West Sussex Gazette* commented wryly, 'It has caught the complaint of unpunctuality from its neighbour'. As the train came into Chichester, it was reported that 'handkerchiefs were waved by ladies from the windows', and that some of the onlookers were watching from the roof of the gasworks.

The *Chichester Observer*, on the following Wednesday, described it as a 'momentous event ... to shareholders and inhabitants. Signs of pleasure and delight were manifested by flags hung at available points, inhabitants giving cheers as it passed'. It went on to eulogise over the rolling stock, 'three handsomely decorated cars of corridor pattern, exceedingly well-built. The seating accommodation is on the style of the top of London buses, each seat accommodating two persons with central aisle. They are of pitchpine and the interior with the large windows is most pleasing and attractive'. Two cars contained room for 48 persons, the third having a luggage compartment where the guard, doubling up as conductor, would be based. The *Observer* also mentioned the freight stock, six open goods trucks with brake van. The report went on to say:

> After many years the greatly desired and needed railway from Chichester through an
> important agricultural district to the growing seaside resort of Selsey is a fait accompli.
> In no part of the country has a proper means of communication with a railway centre
> been more longed for. In these days when time means money, something better than
> carrier traffic was required, not only for the needs of the agriculturists in Sidlesham and
> Manhood, but more especially for Selsey which every year is becoming more popular to
> those who need a quiet holiday by the sea. The transit of goods was an expensive and
> laborious matter whilst the conveyance of a rapidly increasing number of visitors and
> residents is an ever more irksome and very inconvenient matter.

The paper pointed out that the 'necessary cohesion between landlords and promoters',
in other words, the avoidance of an Act of Parliament or Light Railway Order, was
only achieved 12 or 18 months before. It also openly stated that, although the line
had been constructed under the Tramways Act, to all intents and purposes it was a
light railway without the usual expenses of promoting a Bill. The line cost £19,000 to
construct, £7,000 of this coming from debentures – somewhat less than the £75,000
which the 1888 scheme would have cost!

When the train drew in a bouquet was presented to the mayoress, then all eyes
turned to the mayor whose pleasant duty it was to declare the line open. He
reminded the crowd of the 'ambitious but painful bashful young lawyer' who
attempted to deliver an address at the opening of a railway bridge but 'got beautifully
mixed and said the spot on which they stood 'was a howling wilderness and he hoped
would remain so'. 'I would not liken', the mayor continued, 'the site on which the
station now stands as a howling wilderness but as a mild and peaceful meadow where
lambs had frolicked and beasts had grazed'. Dutiful laughter followed. 'The forma-
tion of the tramway might be the means of a great deal of comfort and prosperity to
both Selsey and Chichester', he continued, to hearty applause. 'I won't take up any
more of your time', he said. 'I know you will wish to partake of the good things provided at the other end of the line.' More laughter greeted this reference to the lunch
that had been laid on at Selsey, and which presumably by this time was set down on
the table.

The mayor then invited the assembled company to take their seats, and he proceeded to mount the engine, speaking of this present occasion being 'the commencement of far more important things'. Then, one imagines to the consternation
of Tim Johnson, the driver, he announced, 'I am now going to indulge in one of the
greatest happinesses I had conceived as a boy, that of driving the engine'. He then
declared the line open, to vociferous cheering, joined in by spectators in the meadow
opposite. At 1.57 p.m., exploding fog signals told the world that the first official rail
conveyance between Chichester and Selsey was on its way. Whether or not the mayor
did actually take the controls is something that will never be known – rumour states
that he did indeed do so, the *West Sussex Gazette* hastening to point out that 'no-one
jumped from their cars with astonishment, such was the confidence he inspired'.
Others believe that all he did was sound the whistle – an opinion borne out by one of
the lunch guests (see below). What is certain is that at the drawbridge shortly before
Hunston he quitted the post, and returned to the saloon to enjoy the salutes of the
passers-by in comparative comfort.

The official maiden traverse of the peninsula by train brought with it some colourful description. The *Observer* reporter remembers the 'circular sweep through the meadows', the 'large fields and verdant hedgerows', the 'men busily engaged in harvesting operations', and the skirting of the canal with 'cattle browsing on the banks'. The *Gazette* man wrote of the scene at Hunston where, although there was a siding, 'the station site is as yet given over to cocks and hens: the oldest inhabitant was observed looking wonderingly as Puffing Billy still kept on his wild career to the south'.

One unofficial stop was made at the drawbridge, to enable Councillor Fielder to get out and take a snapshot from the towpath. This was not the only distinguishing feature of the journey; flags and bunting lined the route, and at Kipson Bank Windmill, just south of Hunston, the sails were decorated with streamers. Special mention should be made of the scene at Sidlesham where a number of villagers greeted the train with a cheer, 'among them', wrote the *Observer*, 'Mrs. Stevens, an old lady of eighty six summers, who, seated in a basket chair, appeared delighted at the novel spectacle'. Another commentator pointed out that this same Mrs. Stevens was alive at the time of the Battle of Waterloo! – an example of the crossing of the bridges of time. Selsey, too, was en fête for the occasion, with fluttering flags awaiting the train's arrival. Vehicles were in attendance for the ladies: the remainder of the passengers proceeded on foot to the marquee erected at Beacon House for the champagne

3. Beacon House, Selsey, *c.*1910, scene of the reception to mark the opening of the line.

celebration lunch. It must have felt like high tea. 'As it was now past three', reported the *Gazette*, 'no-one required pressing to sit down to the very choice repast which the hospitality of Mr. Grafton and the directors had provided'.

The meal certainly was choice, consisting of Selsey's 'unrivalled lobsters and prawns, and wines from the *Dolphin Hotel*'. It was reported that apologies had been sent from Lord Edmund Talbot M.P., and Sir Robert Raper, 'called to Petersfield on important business'. Once again it fell to Alderman Ballard to address those present.

The mayor regarded the day as marking an 'epoch in the history of Selsey'. He acknowledged that it was virtually the only railway that had been constructed so cheaply. The idea he said was to facilitate the transit of agricultural goods between Chichester and Selsey, and the transit of passengers: the need had long been felt. 'I am not quite sure', he said, 'that it is an unmixed blessing: Selsey is beautifully isolated and it is a great advantage for busy men to come down, lie still and do nothing, not troubled very much by letters, telegrams and such things'. He acknowledged, to more laughter, that the aim of the promoters was to convey passengers to and from the coast 'slowly but surely', as well as cheaply. He applauded the 'pluck and perseverance' of the directors and officials, and reckoned that with the train, even accounting for its slow speed, people could reach Selsey more quickly than if they drove and perhaps far more safely. Much laughter greeted his assertion that the directors 'would probably not feel it necessary to provide sleeping or dining cars', and he hoped 'passengers could survive without recourse to the refreshment room'. He hoped that the trains would be punctual and would thereby set an example to the London, Brighton and South Coast Railway, whose opening, some 50 years before, he was able to recall. He described Selsey as having become a 'rising and fashionable watering place' and was delighted at the opportunity to run from Chichester to the sea without 'the abominable nuisance of waiting about at Barnham Junction'. Modern day travellers from Chichester to Bognor might well subscribe to the same sentiments! Indeed it was reported exactly a week later in the *Chichester Observer* that passengers travelling from Chichester to Bognor by the 10.27 a.m. train were delayed at Barnham for over an hour and got to Bognor at 12.25 p.m. The promoters of the Selsey line, anxious to see beachlovers flock to Selsey, must have been delighted!

A toast was proposed and drunk, and the chairman at the table, one of the share-holders, responded. 'I believe', he said, 'that the new undertaking might do a great deal – it will bring customers to market, and will get people down from town to spend their money'. He stated that the success of the line would depend very largely on the co-operation and patronage of the local landowners. He applauded the 'honesty and economy' with which the work had been carried out, everything having been 'done efficiently at minimal cost', providing an incentive to other districts to start similar railways. 'I must confess', he said, 'I had a momentary alarm when I heard that the Mayor of Chichester was going to drive the train', raising a few smiles, 'and it was with feelings of considerable thankfulness that I heard that the engine driver would not let him do anything more than blow the whistle'. This statement was greeted with more laughter and some applause and there was even greater applause when a Mr. Fletcher rejoiced that the tramway had brought the main line in touch with 'that rising watering place which for healthfulness and beauty of landscapes and above all its sea views is unrivalled, in my opinion, along the south coast'. Sadly there was little time after the meal to enjoy this scenery because the train was waiting to convey the mayoral party back to Chichester.

Next day the line opened to the public and it is reported that Mr. H. H. Moore paid the first shilling for the line, being one of 96 passengers to do so.

The tramway soon became an established and accepted part of the Manhood scene, and reaction to it was, on the whole, very favourable, serving, as one commentator said, 'both residents and visitors at a time when there was little or no alternative transport'. The *Hampshire Telegraph* was so impressed that it went so far as to suggest that a separate link line should be built allowing through trains from Brighton and Worthing to Selsey. Whitechurch, writing in the *Railway Magazine* soon after its opening did not go that far, but stated that 'Farmers have appreciated the new method of locomotion for the transit of produce, whilst the inhabitants of the villages, who were wont to spend half a day in a carrier's cart on their way to market, must find the new method of journeying to Chichester a great boon'. If the fares were lowered, he pointed out, and the service was good, the people of Chichester would be eager to take advantage of the facilities offered: the little light railway would have a splendid chance of giving the Chichester people what they had been wanting for years – a short, easy route to the seaside, with an opportunity for those with two or three hours to spare, to enjoy a sea-dip and a breath of pure ozone. 'I wouldn't be surprised', he wrote, 'to see a bill advertising a special excursion from Selsey to London. One looks forward to its development with interest. Though I may have raised a laugh at its expense, I heartily wish it every success'. It is interesting that having paid a shilling for his single journey, he should state that the fares should be lowered: one reason for the financial collapse of the company was that the fares were too low.

The company did not commit itself to arrival times during the first few weeks: a subsequent timetable was 'merely to set a time before which trains will not start', but in due course timetables were drawn up. The Selsey Beach extension was completed and opened in 1898, and the remaining work, incomplete at the time of opening, was duly carried out. And so began a most unusual and colourful piece of English railway history.

Chapter Two

Colonel Stephens

Colonel Holman Frederick Stephens was one of the most remarkable entrepreneurs the railway industry has ever had in this country. It was he who was appointed engineer of the tramway, and thereby added yet another line to what was to become quite a substantial empire of mostly country railway routes, all with a distinctive character of their own. A book about the Selsey Tram, called 'undoubtedly the most rustic of all Colonel Stephens' lines', would not be complete without a study of this unique man.

Holman Stephens was born in Hammersmith, London on 31 October 1868. His father was well-known for his membership of the pre-Raphaelite Brotherhood, a group of painters, and was an art critic for the *Athenaeum.* Holman himself was educated at University College School and on the continent, but even before this he

4. Driver Johnson poses with railmen King, Barnes and Gilbert at Chichester station, *c.* 1906.

5. Luther Clayton, one of the first of the Tramway's directors, pictured here *c*.1897.

6. Luther Clayton and James Clayton, off duty, *c*.1897.

used to enjoy sitting in his nursery, surrounded by primitive model rolling stock and track. He matriculated at the University of London in 1887 and in 1888 he became apprenticed at the Metropolitan Railway Company's works at Neasden – hardly the most auspicious start to any career! His father encouraged him in his work, as is seen by the letter he sent to Holman's boss in July 1890:

> I have waited for an opportunity to thank you very warmly indeed for your great kindness in allowing my son to enter the Company's workshop at Neasden, and work there for a considerable time. I hope that those under whom you gave him opportunities of learning his profession found my son energetic, practical and teachable. I should regard it an additional favour if a certificate of his having worked at Neasden could be granted to him.

In 1890 Holman started a remarkable career of light railway management and acquisition: without exception they were independent of the established railway companies. The railways were characterised by their corrugated iron buildings, sharp curves and multiplicity of level crossings. From then until his death in 1931, he involved himself in the construction and management of at least 15 different railways, and he promoted a number of others which failed to come to fruition. Stephens set up his headquarters at 23 Salford Terrace, Tonbridge, a mid-terrace building sandwiched between shops. The only break he took from his railway management was during the First World War, when at the age of 46 he volunteered for the Territorial Reserves, and rose to the rank of Lieutenant Colonel in 1916. From this time he became known simply as 'the Colonel'. Having returned to civilian life, he continued to control his empire until 1931 when, after a series of strokes, he died at the *Lord Warden Hotel*, Dover, eight days before his 63rd birthday. The Colonel had never married, and he left no surviving relatives. During his lifetime he owned or rented a number of properties, including ones in Hammersmith, Robertsbridge, Dover and Tonbridge. He belonged to some London clubs and various professional institutions. His only other interest besides railways was Classical Greek and Roman Mythology – one of the locomotives on the tramway was named the *Hesperus*. After Stephens' death his lines deteriorated, many going bankrupt and all of them closing. Little trace remains of them today. He was respected by all on the Selsey tramway who worked for him: his 'common touch' is illustrated by the cheque for £2 he gave Ganger Skinner, who worked on the tramway, for a new set of teeth, with an accompanying note saying, 'I hope they will be a success'. On other lines, particularly in Wales, he commanded less respect.

Whatever may have happened to his lines after his death, Stephens was universally acclaimed as a champion of the small railway. Turner describes him as 'one of the most extraordinary personages ever in the history of the railways of these islands'; Boyd called him 'the king of minor railways', saying that the Colonel had achieved 'a particular notoriety and fame because of the number of bucolic and decrepit undertakings with which he was connected'; he was described by a former employee as 'a man ahead of his time'; Scott-Morgan called him 'one of the most fascinating administrators in Britain's railway history'.

7. The beautiful view just south of Sidlesham which travellers would have enjoyed, pictured *c*.1908. A goods train proceeds southwards from Sidlesham. This section of the track can now be walked and indeed is part of a nature trail.

Whilst in 1923 most of Britain's railways were merged into the 'big four' group of companies, the Stephens' railways formed an unofficial fifth group, not allowing themselves to be incorporated. They were ruled with a rod of iron from the office in Tonbridge: some were ramshackle affairs Stephens took over from former owners, while he created others himself. Stephens was clever at running the basic railway with minimal expenses and frills, simply coping with what material there was to hand. He practised strict economies on all the lines, most of the locomotives being mainline cast-offs or secondhand industrial engines. Stephens disliked scrapping equipment and resented paying water rates, preferring to use windpumps. He often swapped locomotives about on his various lines. He could see that steam was not necessarily the most economic way of running a railway; he could not tolerate the cost of steam locomotives. It was Stephens who was, on this basis, responsible for the introduction of the primitive petrol railbus which was to become a regular feature on the Selsey tramway in its later years, and in this was well ahead of the main companies who had given no thought to the internal combustion engine as a means of traction. For many, the sight of these extraordinary vehicles is an instant reminder of Stephens.

Scott-Morgan eulogises freely about Stephens' railways. They had, he said, 'a deeply human spirit that lacked the humbug and the hypocrisy of the railway rule book'. The lines passed through some of Britain's loveliest countryside:

and as the trains passed along their timeless path, from little stations and sleeper-built halts from dawn to dusk they seemed to take with them the hopes and the dreams of the country folk they served so well – the same local folk who maintained the stations, maintained the track, maintained the fences and operated the trains.

8. Little vegetation featured round the line; this section between Ferry and Selsey was an exception.

Scott-Morgan went on to discuss the great characters of the lines – they were their own bosses, ready with helpful advice whilst not tending the flowers in the station garden. He describes the individuality and independence of the lines 'where people were individuals, and society valued each and every member by what he stood for in himself rather than by sheer materialism'. He describes a journey on a typical Stephens line:

> As the train rumbled and bucketed its way through the darkening evening sky, as the gas lamp flickered, casting long, dark shadows down the compartment, I had a feeling of great contentment, for the day's work was done and it was time to return to nowhere, from whence one had come that morning.

Scott-Morgan might easily have been describing the Selsey tramway, but of course the lines were countrywide, each with its own quaint characteristics and amusing stories. There was the Kent and East Sussex Railway, where the Gents at Bodiam had no w.c. and only a rainwater pipe intended to flush the urinal: in times of drought the smell was unbearable. On the Snailbeach Railway, the foreman refused to obey Stephens' order to overhaul and restore a certain locomotive because he hated it so much. There was the North Devon and Cornwall Junction Railway with stations bearing the names Hole, Dunsbear and Petrockstow. The takings on the Cranbrook and Paddock Wood Railway, Stephens' first project, were boosted by the hop pickers' specials from London on September weekends. The Ashover Light Railway had passenger trains that were worked using open wagons fitted with seats, and locos

named *Peggy* and *Joan*. There was the East Kent line designed to serve collieries in
the area, but only three out of the eight mines achieved commercial working, and a
train on the line was once pelted with rotten eggs and other missiles by a passenger
for whom the train had refused to stop. The Weston, Clevedon and Portishead line
was used for coal storage during the German occupation of France, when the export
of Welsh coal to France had to be suspended. The Edge Hill Light Railway was built
to transport ironstone, which promptly gave out soon after the line opened to traffic.
There was the Ffestiniog Railway – the only one apart from the Kent and East Sussex
which has been revived by enthusiasts – where the Colonel was disliked. If he
dropped in, as he tended to, to see how things were going, drivers would stroke their
beards when trains carrying the Colonel drew into the station, thus tipping off
station staff that he was on the train. Memos sent by the Colonel to the railway
authority were just thrown in the bin. Lastly there was the Rye and Camber tramway,
also in Sussex, constructed without statutory order, where golfers would pull out the
connection between carriages so that the second vehicle was left stranded halfway
down the line. As well as the lines, Stephens had a hand in other projects which were
proposed, including a Surrey and Sussex Light Railway and an Isle of Lewis railway,
in the far north-west.

Colonel Stephens hated photographers and enthusiasts, which is why he would be
amazed and probably displeased to have been immortalised in the small and attractive
town of Tenterden on the borders of Kent and East Sussex. An entire room in the
Tenterden Town Museum, which draws many visitors every year, is given over to

9. The tramway in a cathedral setting, *c*.1910. The spire of the cathedral soars majestically above the
Manhood and its line.

10.   View of Hunston station. Hunston's one-armed station-master, Mr. Gilbert, had a son known as 'Punch' who worked on the line.

Colonel Stephens. It is appropriate that the museum should be so close to the head-quarters of one of the Colonel's railways, the Kent and East Sussex.

The room contains a very large number of exhibits, ranging from letters written by him, to debenture certificates in respect of companies responsible for running the lines he engineered. There are exhibits from all his railways, with photographs, notices, signboards, tickets, a comic postcard, the Colonel's collection of free passes (of which he had 70!) and other memorabilia. There are some especially notable exhibits, including a notice from one of the lines saying 'Passengers are respectfully requested to refrain from SPITTING in the railway carriages', a Cynicus postcard from the Tenterden to Headcorn line which is exactly the same as one drawn from the Selsey tram route, a letter Colonel Stephens wrote to his father in 1901 express-ing pleasure at the increase in traffic on the Selsey tramway (not being affected by coal or labour troubles as their undertakings were so small), a black bag marked 'Brother Holman F. Stephens, Lodge Loyalty and Charity No 1584' and a share cer-tificate for six fully paid £5 shares dated 23 September 1920 in the name of William Henry Austen, whose name was given to an engine. The terms and conditions attached to the Selsey Tram free passes are worthy of comment too, as they exempted the Railway Company from responsibility for, among other things, delay – somewhat ironic in view of the causes of some of the delays (see *Humour on the Tram*). Both 'Ordinary' and 'Saloon' free passes were issued to Stephens. The walls contain, among other things, nameplates of some of the locos on Stephens' lines, including the *Selsey*.

In one corner of the room is an attempt to recreate Stephens' Tonbridge office, with heavy wooden desk overflowing with books – mainly on civil engineering and railways (of course) – postcards, various rubber stamps and other stationery appropriate to the age. There are some framed photographs of locomotives, including one of the *Selsey* and a set of five photographs depicting the 'result of the gale at Selsey' – in other words the 1910 floods which affected an area to the north of Selsey (see *1910 Floods – Harbinger of Doom*). Sadly, access is prevented by a glass partition.

Before leaving Tenterden, it is worth mentioning the Kent and East Sussex Railway again. Unlike the Selsey Tram, the Kent and East Sussex is a preserved line, the track having in 1974 been reopened between Tenterden and Northiam, 20 years after closure. Of course it now primarily serves the tourist trade, and with smartly restored, amply proportioned stations, rails and sleepers in good repair, and an impressive fleet of locomotives and coaches, there is little evidence of the quaintness and indeed economy which characterised Stephens' lines – on the occasion of the writer's visit he was charged over £1 for coffee and biscuits on board! The Colonel Stephens shop, on Tenterden platform, does a roaring trade in Colonel Stephens After Dinner Mints, Colonel Stephens Butterscotch and Colonel Stephens Assorted Toffee, but has precious little material on the tramway. The 'Collector's Carriage' in a nearby field had no such material at all when this writer visited.

It is hardly surprising that a line engineered by a man with zest for economy and with an eye to the needs of the remoter communities should reflect Stephens' traits in that it was run with great economy, at the ultimate cost of human life, and did not pretend to serve concentrated urban areas. Without the entrepreneurial skills of Stephens, one is left to wonder how differently the tramway's history, particularly the proposed Wittering extension and the introduction of the railbuses, might have had to be written. Throughout its brief life, the tramway had the Stephens flavour and is a worthy part of the collection of 'Colonel Stephens Railways' which will for ever be remembered as standing apart from the mainstream of railways in Britain in their uniqueness and jealously-guarded independence.

One cannot leave this chapter on an amazing man without quoting David St John Thomas:

> No new piece of equipment was ever purchased, if anything second-hand would do. Sheer devotion succeeded where formal management was lacking, and if the traffic did not provide enough for the week's wages he dipped into his own pocket. The Colonel would arrive unexpectedly, order a special and make an inspection, cigars being handed out to the staff if all was well, blistering memos following if not. Not one of the lines is now with us; the public mocked the Colonel Stephens' lines and anything run cheaply enough to make economic sense. Tall, with dipped moustache, bowler hat and cane, he had a distinct military bearing, and though he could be kind he was not always loved. Apart from military service, his whole life was devoted to this curious string of semi-derelict lines: the more rural the surroundings the greater the challenge.

Chapter Three

Construction, Finance and Legal Background

Construction
To say that the line was constructed economically is a huge understatement. The track itself, physically connected to the main line by an awkward junction, consisted of standard sleepers to which were spiked flat-bottomed rails. One hundred men were employed to lay the line, which was completed within four months. There was a slight delay owing to a brief strike caused by the contractor lowering the men's wages by a halfpenny per hour. The construction was rough, and in the final years the joints were found to have been badly aligned, making for an extremely noisy uncomfortable ride. In places the track was submerged under weeds two to three feet high. The gauge was the same as for the main Chichester-Brighton line of 4ft. 8½ in. and the rails were designed to bear around 45 lbs. per yard, similar to those used in the U.S.A. and Canada. There was little in the way of ballast, what there was containing sea-shingle and gravel. Little attention was paid to constructing a level bed and the line closely followed the undulating surface.

11. All aboard at Chichester.

18

The line had precious few other adornments. There were no crossing gates and there was no signalling, merely a telephone link between stations. If a train broke down on the line, it would be necessary to send a boy on to each station to tell intending passengers that there were to be no further trains that day. The terrain was flat, never higher than 50 ft., the steepest gradient being 1 in 50 south of Hoe Farm., so there was no need for tunnelling or gradient marks. The track did not double at all, and the nickname 'Hedgerow Railway' arose from the fact that the lines hugged the hedgerows on each side – although there were some sidings and a passing loop. The catch points designed to stop runaway coaches and wagons were totally insecure and the only lineside signs were the 5 m.p.h. speed reduction boards. Perhaps the only other thing of note concerning the line itself was a profusion of curves which was remarkable considering the flatness of the terrain; the sharpest curve was of six chains radius, just outside Chichester station.

The one highlight, in railway engineering terms, was the impressive drawbridge over the canal just north of Hunston. Indeed it was likened by one writer to the

12.   Railmen Skinner, Hellyer, Cosens, Sprouce, Wackford and others working on the line at the point of its most pronounced curve, just outside Chichester station, c.1920. This area of track remained in position until 1947.

13. The tramway's outstanding feat – the Hunston lift-bridge.

14. A tramway driver's view of the Hunston lift-bridge

drawbridge of an early feudal castle. This was owned by Chichester Corporation, who charged £2 per annum for its use. Before the bridge was completed there was no way of transporting any locomotives from the north to the south side of the canal and, in order to move the *Chichester* engine to the south side, the railwaymen laid pieces of track on the road, which were then taken up after the train had passed over them and replaced further down! Water had to be pumped out in order that the foundations could be laid. To operate the bridge special winching tackle was provided, but on one occasion the bridge refused to be lowered, stopping traffic for several days. It is reported somewhat pessimistically, that, a barge was kept under the bridge during its first few weeks of operation to catch the train if the bridge gave way! It was in fact the delay in completing the bridge which held up the opening of the line itself; in 1924 the bridge was declared closed, and remained fixed for the rest of the life of the line. A drawbridge had been necessary in view of the small sailing ships which had used the canal. There were no parapets: any railway staff needing to cross on foot had to jump between the cross girders or risk a tightope walk along the railhead. Construction began early in 1897 under Colonel Stephens' supervision. In 1932 Klapper reported that the winching equipment 'had not been called upon for many years', and by 1934 commercial usage of the canal had ceased altogether, which was not surprising in view of the new road bridge which together with the railway bridge presented an impenetrable obstruction to eastbound craft. It is reported that the

15.   A modest assembly of passengers at Chichester station. The cathedral and main station can be seen in the background.

16. A tramway journey has just started from Chichester, hauled by the *Selsey* in April 1911.

bridge was blown up upon the outbreak of the Second World War to prevent use by an invading army. The only other bridges to be seen on the route were the bridge over the line at Selsey, giving its name to one of a trio of stations in Selsey, and a simple timber construction over a channel just north of Ferry Station at Pagham harbour edge, standing on crumbling concrete abutments containing marine shingle.

The stations were virtually all built with concrete faced platforms, but there were few other unifying features. Each station apart from the halts at Mill Pond and Golf Club had sidings, but no stations were staffed except Chichester, Selsey Town and Hunston. There was a building of sorts at each station except Hoe Farm, Mill Pond and Golf Club, the buildings in the main being timber-framed and clad with galvanised iron on concrete foundations, although Ferry could only boast a small wooden shed for shelter. Gaslights were provided at Chichester and Selsey Town, oil illumination elsewhere.

Chichester, the northern terminus, had a station building and platform quite separate from the main-line station: it was necessary for those arriving at Chichester from Midhurst, Portsmouth or London to walk down Stockbridge Road for their Selsey connection. This was to prove most harmful to the tramway when the buses began operating (see *Chapter 10*). However, although there were no through trains from the branch to the main line or vice versa, there were runaround facilities and,

17.   The station at Hunston.

18.   The tramway's water-stop at Hunston seen here in 1932, with *Morous*.

19 & 20. The station at Chalder.

21. What remains of Chalder station today.

as has been mentioned, a connection with the main line. Appropriately enough, the station backed on to the rear end of the gardens of houses in Terminus Road, situated to the south of the main line. The most prominent sight confronting travellers arriving at Chichester from Selsey was the enormous gasworks almost directly opposite.

The first stop out of Chichester was Hunston, mistakenly referred to by Cooke in his book *Off the Beaten Track* as 'Donnington'. Hunston was the cooling and watering depot. Next was Hoe Farm, a private halt, with a siding provided for farm users in consideration of the conveyance of the relevant land to the company: an example of the operation of the 'back-scratching' principles at work in the foundation of the line. Chalder followed, on a private farm road, the company paying the landowners £2 per annum for its use by passengers. Mill Pond Halt was the next stop. Rush in April 1935 reported 'letters in all manner of incongruous positions (on the sign-board) and in consequence ... difficult to read'. These last three stops were all in fairly remote surroundings, the names coming from nearby habitations. At length Sidlesham, named after the straggling village, was reached, situated at the southern extreme of the village on the edge of the harbour (reclaimed as land at the time of opening), and not far from the Methodist chapel. In the early days it was spelt 'Siddlesham' on the nameboard, reflecting its pronunciation although this was later rectified. Ironically, Chalder was much closer to the village church and pub! Follow-ing the 1910 floods the station building was lifted and replaced at right angles to the track, and the signboard was again replaced – with the correct spelling this time! At the other end of the harbour was the next stop, Ferry, with just a short wooden platform, consisting of a few sleepers piled together, and the modest wooden shelter. Golfers were well served by the next station, Golf Club Halt, opened some time later, again private and not recognised by the Bradshaw timetable until 1913. The *Chichester Observer* in 1908 commented that 'It is gratifying to note that the Chichester and Selsey Tramway authorities intend to afford facilities to players by making a halt at the links'. The course was originally 18 holes but was reduced in 1917 to 12 under the Wartime (Cultivation of Land) Order.

The line ended with the three 'Selsey' stations – Bridge, Town and Beach. Bridge, with a private siding for the Trojan Brickworks and the Company's ballast pit, was unremarkable although it reminds one of the only 'overbridge' on the line. Town contained the headquarters of the tramway company and became the terminus after the closure of Beach. It was not in fact finished in time for the opening but when completed it boasted a waiting room, a booking office and a superintendent's office, while the platform was later lengthened. Rush commented that the existence of a petrol pump outside the running shed at Selsey Station gave it the appearance of a garage! It was considered fortunate that the station was towards the east end of the village, regarded as less wealthy than the inhabitants of West Beach, the population of the east being less likely to afford other means of transport. Beach was opened on 1 August 1898, its opening being confined to the summer months only, and brought closer to the sea each year by coastal erosion. It ceased to be used shortly before the First World War, Mr. Heron-Allen believing that regular usage ceased in 1905. In 1963 the remains of the old platform, between the beach and the fishermen's huts, could still be discerned.

22. Sidlesham station before the flood, with misspelt signboard and would-be passengers. It was the only intermediate station with passing loop and 'up' and 'down' platforms.

23. Sidlesham before the flood, the nameboard now correctly spelt, *c.*1908.

24.   A view of Sidlesham station, pre-1910, from near the *Crab and Lobster Inn*.

25.   Sidlesham station, after the 1911 reconstruction, showing that the waiting room had been moved at right angles to the tracks, so that it had its back to the prevailing winds. This picture was taken in 1935.

26 & 27. Two views of the primitive facilities offered at Ferry Station.

By 1913, the tramway was thriving and, like any thriving enterprise, it was inevitable that expansion would be proposed. The obvious choice seemed to be an extension to the Witterings. Just nine years before, E. V. Lucas in his *Highways and Byways of Sussex* wrote that 'A tramway between Chichester to Selsey has to some extent opened up the eastern side of the peninsula, but the west is still remote, and will probably remain so'. There

28. For golfers only – the modest Golf Links Halt. In 1930 it is said that a golfer tried to knock the engine down with his car and came off second best!

was no doubt that the tram had brought more people to Selsey, providing the only regular, fast route from Chichester to the foot of the peninsula. The theory, which seemed unassailable, was that a similar scheme would bring the same prosperity to the Witterings – that East Wittering would in turn develop as a seaside resort and this would encourage more people to visit it by train.

There was one major snag: the Selsey Tramway had been constructed without any parliamentary sanction at all. The land had been acquired privately, thereby obviating the necessity of obtaining a Light Railway Order carrying with it powers of compulsory purchase. With the Wittering extension compulsory purchase orders would be necessary, therefore a Light Railway Order would have to be sought. Since such a step was unavoidable it was decided to kill two birds with one stone, and seek some measure of legality for the Selsey Tramway which had always been lacking, by obtaining a Light Railway Order to enable the existing route to be reconstructed, in accordance with the legal requirements for railways.

The chairman of the company announced the proposed application at the 1913 A.G.M. stating that the opening of the new route would be of great benefit to the inhabitants: the company, he said, owed the local public a duty to be the 'first in the field' as far as providing acceptable public transport for them was concerned. He acknowledged that at that time the tramway company was 'responsible to no-one', confirming the lack of parliamentary approval or indeed sanction for the tramway, but saw that under the proposed order legality would be obtained, and the confidence of the travelling public thereby secured.

29.   Passengers passing the time of day at Selsey. Perhaps it was easier to leave the billboards on the ground than attach them to the corrugated iron.

The proposal was an ambitious one, and involved three separate stretches of track. The first stretch consisted of an arm off the existing tramway, leaving the tramway at Hunston and proceeding to Birdham. A second stretch would proceed to the Witterings, while a third, branching off at Birdham, would proceed to Itchenor. It was hoped that the order would also allow a link line at the parting of the Selsey Tramway and the Wittering extension: it was envisaged that the communities of Appledram, Birdham, East and West Wittering, Shipton Green and Itchenor would all be served. At West Itchenor it was proposed that a 200-ft. long pier would be built and vessels weighing up to 800 tons would be received there. The estimated cost of the project was just under £81,000.

The scheme did not receive universal approval, and accordingly it was necessary to hold a public inquiry. Colonel Stephens attended the inquiry to put the case for the company. He pointed out that the capital had been raised locally for the tramway, and the fact that the takings had averaged £10 per mile per week, a very good figure considering the shortness of the tramway, boded well for a proposed extension. The reconstruction work, he explained, would consist of relaying the line and resignalling, with swing bridges and gates to be erected. Stephens then talked about the extension. It would, he said, run parallel with the Chichester Canal for two miles, then south-west past Birdham until it was a quarter of a mile from Shipton Green: at that point a branch to Itchenor would be constructed. The 200-ft. long concrete jetty at Itchenor, by the Custom House, would cost £2,500. The Witterings, said Colonel Stephens, to which the south-west extension would run, had 'an excellent front of sand'. The scheme was calculated 'to add another seaside resort to the south coast'. The whole scheme would involve the erection of five stations.

Colonel Stephens' two principal supporters at the inquiry were Mr. Phillips and Mr. Heron-Allen. Mr. Phillips pointed out that much seaborne traffic was to be expected from West Itchenor, with a considerable amount of agricultural produce. Traffic on the tramway had also increased. Mr. Heron-Allen assured the inquiry that there would be no great difficulty in financing the undertaking.

30.   The trackbed at Stockbridge crossing, looking north, 1932.

A number of people objected to the application. A Mr. Wyatt complained that land belonging to the Oliver Whitby Trust would be interfered with. A Mr. Harris said he would oppose it, unless the company undertook to erect a station at Donnington! A Mr. Mason stated that the extension would cut up some property very considerably, and would spoil a good deal of prospective building land. An objection was also raised by Westhampnett Rural District Council. They regarded it as necessary for public safety that the company should be required to erect and maintain gates across the railways on each side of the road at five of the level crossings, and make provision for the crossings to be lit at night.

The presence and proximity of the Chichester Canal also gave rise to some objection. The county surveyor stated that in his opinion it was dangerous for the extension of the tramline to come within 50 yards of the canal bridges. There were also complaints raised at the inquiry concerning delays to barges through the existence of the present bridge over the Selsey Tramway: on some occasions, barges had been kept waiting on the canal for 45 minutes. It was remarked that there had been an extraordinary increase in passenger traffic.

Supporting the scheme, a Mr. Hogben claimed that at East Wittering there was about six miles of sand on the seashore, and the railway would tend towards development and exploitation of this marvellous facility. A Mr. Arnell reminded the inquiry

31. The *Sidlesham* crossing Hunston lift-bridge, photographed in 1900.

that, before the tramway opened, Selsey had been a place of fishermen and agricultural labourers. Now the tramway had come it had grown rapidly. There would be commercial advantages to the extension, and the public would benefit. Finally the Rev. Preb. W. F. Shaw told the inquiry that he did not think it right 'in these enlightened days' that a light railway should be allowed to pass over the roads so much. He felt that it would deter motorists from using the roads on the basis that they did not like stopping at crossings! The chairman replied that it was in fact Parliament's intention to facilitate the construction of light railways – presumably at the expense of the motorist. It was ironic that it was to be the motor car which was to bring about the downfall of the tramway company!

In spite of the somewhat unwise assertion by Mr. Heron-Allen at the inquiry that he 'did not know the mind of the average countryman', the chairman decided that a

Light Railway Order should be granted. He felt that there was no objection which could not be met in the ordinary way by compensation.

The Light Railway Order was duly granted in the terms sought; this included not only the proposed extensions to Birdham, Itchenor and the Witterings, both East and West, but also allowed the company to 'purchase or lease, reconstruct or repair, renew, work and maintain the existing tramway between Chichester and Selsey'. The Order stated that the company's powers of compulsory purchase should cease after three years from commencement of the order, and that works should be completed within five years. R. W. Rush recalls a timetable headed 'Chichester and Selsey section' possibly with the proposed Wittering section in mind. With the granting of the Order a wave of optimism spread over the operators. It was hoped that sufficient capital could be raised to make it 'an important railway instead of a small tramway' and 'an extremely valuable and important property'.

Unfortunately the scheme was overtaken by events. Before the order was granted, the First World War broke out. Inevitably, government departments geared themselves to the needs of war and less important matters had to take a back seat. The Light Railway Order was not granted until 1915, and because of the war it was allowed to lapse. The extension, so carefully planned and so vigorously campaigned

32. Mill Pond Halt, seen here in early 1911, where trains affected by the 1910 floods had to terminate.

33.   The first of the trio of stations at Selsey, Bridge Halt.

for, never took place. It is doubtful whether, even if it had gone through, it would have saved the Selsey Tramway: one is tempted to the conclusion that it would have become an additional millstone round the company's neck. Nor did the reconstruction take place and therefore in that respect too the Order lapsed. It was not until 1924 that an order was sought to legalise operations, and by that time the tramway was in decline.

The Witterings remain very much like Selsey – large, sprawling villages on the edge of the Manhood Peninsula, just one road connecting them with the rest of civilisation. Itchenor has become an exclusive sailing centre. West Wittering has become an extremely popular seaside spot, with miles of sandy beaches and crowds of motorists flocking to visit them on summer weekend mornings. East Wittering, now linked directly with Bracklesham Bay, is a populous but genteel village with attractive shops and a little promenade of its own. The A286, with a good bus service, provides the link with the rest of the country. One would love to think that, in more environmentally conscious days, there might once more be demand for a railway to the Witterings, and that a skilful entrepreneur could succeed where Colonel Stephens failed.

34.   A sunlit Selsey station, 1918.

35.   A sunny day at Selsey station.

Despite the fact that the powers as set out in the Light Railway Order in relation to the tramway had lapsed in 1920, efforts were made again in 1924 to enable the tramway to operate legally as a railway. It was found that this could be done by means of a little-known, and little-used Act, the Railway Construction Facilities Act of 1864. Its purpose was to cheapen applications for legal power to run railways where compulsory purchase of land was not necessary. With the aid of this Act some lines had acquired legal status, among them the railway linking Epsom Mental Hospital in Surrey with the main line, with the consequent unflattering nickname, the Lunatic Railway! However, the Act had previously only been used three times. The application, if granted under the Act, would give no additional powers: it was merely giving the Board of Trade's blessing to an existing operation.

The only potential obstacle to the grant of a certificate under the 1864 Act was an objection based on the lack of provision of proper crossings. A letter had been presented to Westhampnett Rural District Council in August 1923 calling attention to the dangerous condition of Stockbridge Crossing. This led to the council demanding that crossing gates be provided, so it was necessary to hold a public inquiry. At this inquiry it was pointed out that in one seven-day period in August 1923, 3,840 motor vehicles, 365 horse drawn vehicles and about 2,500 pedal cycles used the Chichester to Selsey road, and that road traffic had more than doubled in recent years. A Mr. Annis, a building surveyor, said he had had several narrow escapes at crossings. Another problem was the continual warning whistling of the tram engine as it approached the crossing. The secretary of the company wondered if a solution would be for the trams to pull up before each crossing.

On 15 July 1924 the certificate was issued and the line at last achieved legality as a railway. The certificate authorised the incorporation of the West Sussex Railway Company, the construction, maintenance and repair of a railway seven miles and four furlongs in length on the lines of the Selsey Tramways between Chichester and Selsey, and the takeover by the new company of the Hundred of Manhood and Selsey Tramway Company once agreement had been reached. The line was renamed the West Sussex Light Railway, and operations were brought under the scope of the Ministry of Transport. Regulations were made regarding the maximum axle loads and speeds, and the new company was empowered to make an agreement with the Southern Railway Company with regard to the reconstruction, working and management of the line. The company was not required to erect gates at crossings unless instructed to do so by the Ministry of Transport.

In October 1928 agreement was reached for the takeover, reconstruction and maintenance of the undertaking of the tramway company by the railway company, as well as assumption of all debts and liabilities. The takeover apparently never took place. The Ministry of Transport did intervene in 1932 concerning rules to be followed at crossings. Other than that, the certificate made little difference to the character or the running of the line. The fact that it was not legally a railway did not sway the Southern Railway in favour of taking it on, which it is suggested might have been a reason for asking for the certificate in the first place.

Finance

The tramway was registered as a limited liability company in 1896 with a nominal share capital of £12,000. This was increased to £16,800 in 1899. By 1934, £2,400 had still not been issued. The balance was raised by means of £7,000-worth of debentures; a further £5,000-worth of debentures were issued between 1911 and 1924. The total construction and land purchase cost was £21,750, a saving of £2,000 having been effected by buying land at less than the going rate, with £3,268 being spent on rolling stock. Some land was obtained at £10 per acre which was regarded even at that time as inexpensive. Running expenses, which of course included not only wages but rents, came to nearly £1,200 per annum. The 1910 floods, which will be considered in more detail later, set the company back £2,500. Up to August 1910 the expenditure was: land construction £20,260 17s. 5d.; rolling stock £3,268 14s. 9d.; and freehold property £1,311 6s. 5d.

Revenue came from a number of sources, passenger fares being just one, others including cottage rents and advertising plates. As we shall see later, there were a number of business customers.

Indeed in 1933, out of a total income of £2,369 18s. 10d., just £427 9s. 11d. came from passenger receipts, comparing somewhat unfavourably with the £3,912 13s. raised from the same source in 1919, £2,406 14s. in 1921, £1,404 6s. 4d. in 1923 and

36. The picturesque traverse of the harbour edge. Note the state of the trackbed! That, together with the apparent absence of passengers, suggests that this photo was taken late in the tramway's life.

£799 6s. in 1925. Fares were kept extremely low; in 1933 it cost just 8d. to travel from Chichester to Selsey. Of the total income for 1933, around £716 came from goods, £293 from rents, £166 from minerals, £692 from coal and coke, £257 from parcels, £56 from miscellaneous traffic, nearly £7 from season tickets, and insignificant amounts for livestock. It is interesting to note, though, that receipts from sources other than fare-paying passengers rose quite substantially between 1932 and 1933 – by over £100, with only a total annual drop of £400 from 1920, when passenger usage had been much higher.

It would be fair to say that outgoings were kept as low as possible, however. At no stage were crossings – reckoned by many to be essential – erected, nothing was done to improve the state of the line or the rolling stock and thereby the comfort of the passengers, and wages were far from princely: a lad porter got just 13s. per week in the early 1930s, a guard conductor £1 per week, a fireman/labourer £2 per week, and a rail car driver £2 12s. 1d. per week. Locals, though, were not particularly interested in keeping costs down: reports of the Westhampnett Rural District Council in July 1928 show how the tramway company was forced to pay higher rates following an objection to the council's rating apportionment. The roads feeding the tramway, it was said, were nothing but dust in the summer and mud in the winter, owing to the tram traffic. It was pointed out that nothing had been paid towards the frontages of Church Road, Selsey, yet the tram had more use thereof than all the other frontages put together, being an inlet and outlet for goods traffic. The upshot was that the company's contribution to the rates in Church Road was increased by 150 per cent – another burden to shoulder. Despite its efforts at economies, the company could not keep up its obligations to creditors, and its bankruptcy in 1931 came as little surprise.

The picture, then, is one of a line very well blessed with stations, bending over backwards to become a real community line, but whose constructional and financial organisation showed a total lack of awareness of economic reality – particularly with regard to the road competition which would make a mockery of the inadequately maintained lines and rolling stock, and which would be responsible for the line's ultimate end.

Chapter Four

Locomotives and Rolling Stock

According to the *Daily Express* reporter, writing in 1935, the Selsey Tramway had 'about the strangest collection of railway stock in the world'. Baker, writing in *Sussex Villages*, comments that the railway was operated by 'second, third and fourth hand engines and carriages of great antiquarian interest and surprising effectiveness'. The 1934 Southern Railway report stated a different point of view: saying 'the company's rolling stock appears to have little value beyond scrap, judged by southern railway standards'. Even the company admitted in 1919 that its own rolling stock was unreliable, commenting at the A.G.M. of that year on 'very great trouble with engines' and stating they had 'taken the bull by the horns and got a third engine recently' thereby rendering them 'practically safe from the probablility of more breakdowns which were so depressing at the beginning of the year'.

Baker's reference to 'second, third and fourth hand engines' was based on hard evidence. There was only one engine which was built specially for the line and which survived right through the line's existence. The rest were all transferred from other lines, like retired pit ponies being put out to grass, coming to spend their dying years in the company's service. None of the locomotives which worked the line survived to work elsewhere after the tramway closed in 1935.

It is perhaps fitting to start with the specially-built engine, appropriately named *Selsey*, called the pride of the line in its early years. The *Selsey*, a Peckett 2-4-2T, was built in 1897, the year the line opened to traffic. Mitchell and Smith called it a 'popular steed'. Scott-Morgan commented on its 'sparkling brass dome' and Rush on its very long chimney. It was rebuilt in 1899 with larger tanks, modifying the coal bunker. Six months before traffic was withdrawn, the engine's boiler burst, having found to be badly leaking, and following the closure of the tramway it was obvious that its life was over. The *Selsey* was cut up in 1936.

The history of the other locomotives was more colourful. The only other locomotive to grace the tramway in its opening years – no more were acquired until 1907 – was the 'original' *Chichester* to distinguish it from a later locomotive which was also given the name *Chichester*. The original, an 0-4-2T, had already enjoyed 50 years' service, having been built originally as an 0-6-0T for the Great Western Railway, by the Longbottom Railway Foundry at Barnsley. The *Chichester* was used during the tramway's construction and is best remembered for its passage to the southern end by road, with rails being laid specially on the road to accommodate it. The *Chichester* hauled the very first official train on the tramway on its day of opening in August 1897. It was scrapped in 1913. All its life the *Chichester* was plagued with derailments: it was usual to carry re-railing jacks on the locomotive.

The third locomotive to arrive was the *Sidlesham*. This was not quite so aged when it first appeared on the Manhood scene in 1907, having been built 46 years before, being dispatched from the makers on 22 January 1861, as Manning Wardle No. 21.

37. The tramway's proudest locomotive acquisition, the *Selsey*, built specially for the tramway and shown as new, *c.*1897

38. The *Selsey* and crew, photographed in 1900.

39. An elderly quartet – the *Selsey*, *Ringing Rock*, *Sidlesham* and *Chichester II* in 1927.

It went first to T. & J. Charlesworth at Rothwell Haigh Colliery, reputedly there being named *Henrietta*. It was then sold to the East and West Yorks Union Railway, which connected a number of Charlesworth's collieries with the Great Northern. Then it went on to Meakings of Birkenhead before proceeding to the Blagdon Waterworks just outside Bristol. It was extensively rebuilt and overhauled by Hawthorn Leslie & Co. before being acquired by the Selsey Tramway. The engine had a number of interesting features, including a square cornered saddletank which it retained throughout its life, a brass funnel, a copper-topped chimney, very heavy buffers and end balconer which enabled the guard and conductor to move between the vehicles and operate a handbrake if necessary. The *Sidlesham* could be described as a typical Stephens purchase – an antiquated industrial cast-off. It was withdrawn in 1930 and scrapped in 1932.

1912 was to be an active year in the field of locomotive acquisition, with time running out for the original *Chichester*. It seemed likely that the war years, which were to be so prosperous for the tramway, would be entered with just two locomotives. But in 1912 moves were made to purchase a brand new 'Triana type' locomotive from Kerr Stuart. One of the company, named Street, contended 'it is no use buying second hand trash' and urged that the purchase proceed. However, not all of his colleagues were convinced, including Colonel Stephens, who felt that 'a little Kent and East Sussex or Plymouth and Devonport engine would no doubt serve your purpose'. Kerr Stuart, under the impression that an order had been placed, worked night and day to meet the delivery date, but the tramway company, denying through their solicitors that an order had been placed, abandoned the purchase, threatening to refuse to accept the engine if the firm attempted to deliver it. Street admitted he was 'heartily sick of the whole business' and had to concede defeat.

40. The *Chichester*: the locomotive that hauled the first official train on the tramway in 1897.

41. *Chichester* together with crew and wagons, at Chichester.

It was indeed a Plymouth and Devonport engine which was received instead – an 1877 0-4-0ST Neilson engine which was named *Hesperus*. Colonel Stephens was the resident manager of the Plymouth Devonport and South Western junction railway for a time. The locomotive had been the 'odd man out' on the Plymouth line, the only one not to be a Hawthorn Leslie. It had come from the East Cornwall Mineral Railway, converted to standard gauge from 3ft. 6 in. and was used to shunt the yard at Callington at the north end of the Plymouth line, before being sold to Colonel Stephens, who by that time had abandoned his involvement with the Plymouth line. This was not the first locomotive which Stephens named *Hesperus* – a name which, presumably, arose from his interest in Greek mythology. It was scrapped in 1927, three years after it was withdrawn in 1924. It is said that on the Kent and East Sussex Railway there was a spectacular derailment, following which Stephens renamed the derailed engine *Hesperus* to disguise its identity from potentially nervous passengers! However, there is evidence that the loco was called, and marked, *Hesperus*, when it was derailed. One wonders why Stephens should have wished to tempt fate by giving an identical name to an engine on the tramway, especially with its miserably short tramway life of 12 years. Perhaps the automatic linking of the work Hesperus with 'wreck' was another offputting feature.

42. The *Hesperus*, pictured at Selsey in July 1928. The name betrayed Colonel Stephens' interest in classical Greek and Roman mythology. The engine too became a 'wreck'.

43, 44 & 45.   The *Sidlesham* alone, and
with company. The *Sidlesham* carried
passengers through the tramway's busiest
period.

With *Sidlesham, Selsey* and *Hesperus* being the only three locomotives to survive the first three years of the war, a further purchase was thought necessary, and in 1917 an 1883 Manning Wardle 0-6-0ST was acquired. Having left the manufacturers in May 1883, it went to J. C. Billups, Cardiff, named *Vida*. From here it went to Pauling & Co. and ended up with Robert McAlpine, who sold it to Colonel Stephens. There is some suggestion that it saw service in France during the First World War. There was something of a history attached to the name given to the loco when it reached the tramway. The name itself *Ringing Rock*, had been given to a locomotive which began its life on the Maenclochwg Railway in Wales (Maenclochwg meaning Ringing Rock) and which had been transferred to the Kent and East Sussex. That was the train thought to have been derailed with the consequent hasty nameplate transfer to the Selsey Tramway, although as has been said, this suggestion appears to have been discredited. Assuming that it was the *Hesperus* which was derailed, it is unclear why the transfer of nameplates took place. The Selsey Tramway *Ringing Rock* just saw the line itself out, being scrapped shortly after it shut, a wedge hammered into the boiler to prevent further use. The nameplate was preserved however, and can be seen in Chichester Museum to this day.

46. A journey on the line by steam train tended to take longer because of the necessity to pick up and deposit wagons. Here a 'mixed train' is led by the *Sidlesham* near Ferry.

Two years later, in 1919, the company actually did splash out and purchased a 20th-century locomotive, a Hudswell Clarke 0-6-0ST, built in 1903. It came from Naylor Brothers, contractors for the Wembley Exhibition, and was unofficially called *Wembley*, having worked in that area. However, the company, doubtless anxious to maintain a connection between the name and the locality, named this loco *Chichester*. It was this locomotive which was tragically involved in the fatal accident in 1923 that is described more fully later in the book. Despite this, the second *Chichester* was saved and kept going until 1932 when it was scrapped. It is ironic that the newest locomotive should have survived for the shortest time.

In the purchase of its seventh and last engine, the company excelled itself. The *Morous* arrived at the tramway in 1924, 58 years old, a Manning Wardle 0-6-0ST of 1866. It had spent all its life in the Midlands and the Welsh Borders, going first to T. R. Crampton at Fenny Compton before being passed to the Stratford-on-Avon and Midland Junction Railway in 1908 and thence in 1910 to the Shropshire and Montgomeryshire. It is thought to have been named after the Cavalier poet Huw Morus, who spent his life near Glyn Ceiriog in north Wales. The tramway company received it with a patched smokebox door, a cab which was described as ungainly, a dented chimney, and also with the knowledge that the engine had been idle for a number of years before the transfer. Together, with *Ringing Rock*, *Morous* was the only engine to survive the line's closure, although by then, its new coat of paint having weathered away, it was clear that it was virtually at the end of its active life. It was cut up on site in 1936 at Chichester. The *Express* reporter who visited the corrugated iron shed in which the engines were stored, was able to discern the words 'Shropshire and

47. A trio of locomotives, safe in Selsey's store, 1932.

Montgomeryshire Railway' which the weathering of the new paintwork had revealed once again. The sight of this, together with the *Selsey* with its burst boiler, the mournful *Ringing Rock* and the wind-battered shed with half its roof missing was as sad an indictment as any on the short-sightedness of the company in not adopting Street's suggestions and investing in modern, fashionable machinery.

Yet ironically it was on the Selsey Tramway that Colonel Stephens first experimented with a very novel, and potentially economic and efficient, form of rail transport. In the early 1920s, he introduced the Wolseley Sidley railbuses on the line, initially on a trial basis and thereafter into normal service. An accident caused this type to be withdrawn, but in 1923 the first Ford railbuses or railcars arrived, followed in 1925 by the four-cylinder engine Shefflex railbuses assembled by the Shefflex Motor Co. of Tinsley, Sheffield, which had first been tested on the Kent and East Sussex Railway at Rolvenden in 1916. These had one or two highly original features: firstly, they could in seconds be converted into roadbuses, and secondly the seat backs were reversible so the queasier passengers were able to dictate whether they sat with their back to, or facing, the direction of travel! Gradually the railbuses took over from the traditional engines, the company boasting that they reduced journey time by nine minutes, and in the summer of 1934 six of the seven services running from Chichester to Selsey were operated by railbuses. The rides were not comfortable because the joints were badly aligned. The journey was noisy and rough, conversation impossible. Galway Power writing in September 1925, stated:

> For 20 years a steam train served the district faithfully and well but such an antiquated method of conveyance was considered too slow for these hectic days, and Henry Ford came to the rescue. The result is an almost ludicrous but nonetheless effective combination of ancient body and up-to-date machinery and by means of a strange conveyance one bumps merrily along to Chichester or Selsey as the case may be, two Ford standard one ton trucks, engines facing the opposite way rear axle to rear axle, compose this exceedingly strange outfit. When the train arrives at a terminus, the driver descends lever in hand as do the tram-men, and proceeds to the other driving seat ready to start off again, this obviating the necessity of shunting and turning round. He performs these driving duties reclining in a chair similar to those seen in the London parks, turning round now and then to talk to the passengers. The fact that there is a steering column and no wheel adds to the impression of comic opera transport. If the wind is not too strong, one or two open luggage vans are interposed between the two passenger coaches.

Stephens insisted that they were reliable, that they 'kept to time, giving no non-sense' – a view somewhat at variance to the *Express* reporter's assertion that they were of the 'tin lizzie' type. Stephens also saw the railcars as providing good competition with the road motor buses, offering cheaper fares. Notwithstanding the faster, more comfortable bus service which had paralleled the line since 1919, Klapper, who believed the running costs of Shefflexes of just over 3d. per mile to be a world record, wrote in 1932: 'preference for rail travel may be considered an even more practical way of assisting our distressed coal and steel areas than any that have been discussed in the daily press in recent months.

This sort of thinking, combined with Stephens' zest for economy, seemed even greater incentive to use the railbuses as much as possible, and in the latter days of the tramway's operation normal service was indeed carried on by the petrol railcars with three doors, the chassis for each carrying a bus-type body with no lining or lettering, the front vehicle being the propelling agent, the rear one being 'towed dead'.

48.   The red-brick houses of Terminus Road remain, but these rails and *Ringing Rock* have long since disappeared, 1935.

49.   Full steam ahead for the *Ringing Rock* which just survived the line's closure. This picture was taken in 1926, and the driver is H. Davies.

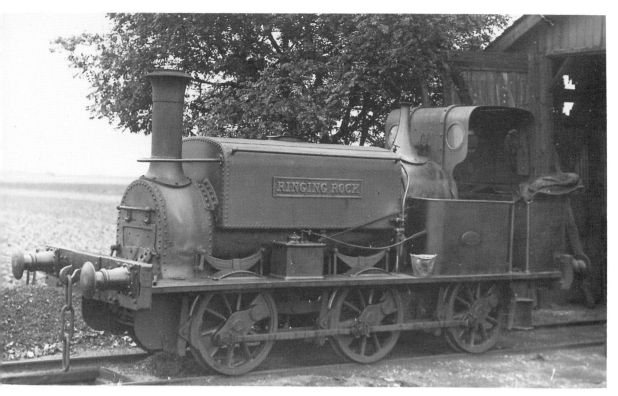

50. *Ringing Rock*, sent in 1917 to join the trio which had seen the tramway's finest hours. This picture dates from July 1927.

51. The Company's prized antique, the *Morous*, nearly 60 years old when it was bought for the tramway.

52. A show of Shefflexes at Selsey,1932.

'Villagers', commented Rush in April 1935, 'seemed to be inured to the roar of the
engine, the exhaust fumes and the bumping and the swaying as the car passed over
the uneven track'.

Passenger accommodation before the advent of the railbuses consisted, like the
engines, of a mixture of carriages built by Falcon and Hurst Nelson specially for the
line, and carriages which had enjoyed substantial use on other lines. One interesting
aspect to this is the occasional appearance of Pullmans and other 'luxury' carriages
on the line, not for regular employment on it, but for transportation to the coast for
their bodies to be converted into holiday homes. Some still exist in Selsey. The
company also accumulated a considerable fleet of wagons and vans from a range of
sources. The specially built carriages, which were attached to the *Selsey* at the line's
beginnings, were known as 'Falcon bogie carriages'. The accommodation therein
ranged from 'uncomfortable looking garden seats', as Nicol put it, in third class, to
more luxurious first class accommodation, some of which consisted of cross benches
for four, and some single corner seats. As well as third and first class compartments, a
compartment was reserved for guard and luggage: Whitechurch recalls his first
impression of the 'Falcon bogies': 'one stood by the little platform ready to start – a
neat, light car on bogies with an entrance at either end and a corridor down the centre with ... three compartments – 'smoking' and, as our German neighbours would
put it 'niet rooken' (*sic*).

53 & 54. Shefflexes with intending passengers, both adult and infant, at Selsey, pictured during the late 1920s.

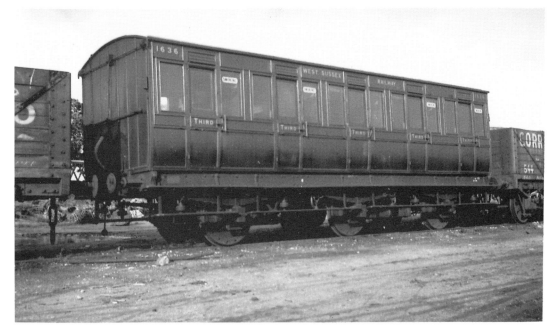

55.   Though never part of the Southern Railway, the tramway was happy to accept its cast-offs. This is a newly acquired six-wheel coach, pictured *c.*1932.

56.   From conveyance to cottage. A tramway carriage begins a new life.

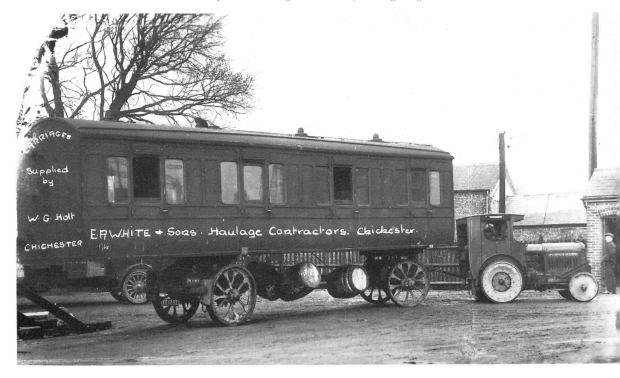

57.   The engine shed at Selsey, this picture was taken prior to 1926, since the domed roof was later replaced by a pitched one.

58.   'How we arrived at Selsey.' Note the fishbaskets and the bicycle. The tramway provided a valuable community service throughout its life.

By 1934 the so-called 'bogies' were, in the words of Southern Railway's report, in 'hopeless condition', as were three of the 'second hand' carriages subsequently purchased. That left three more second-hand carriages ('bad condition') and two six-wheeled carriages which had been purchased from the London, Chatham and Dover line of the Southern Railway. These were reckoned to be the only serviceable carriages in the company's possession, but even these were judged to have 'little value beyond scrap' and a Mr. Doverman, visiting the line around the time of its closure and seeing them, exclaimed, 'it's an old condemned Chatham coach. This can't be safe. Fancy coming all this way to see some of the old scrap running down here'.

It should be remembered that *Ringing Rock* was owned by Colonel Stephens and never owned by the tramway. After Colonel Stephens' death, the *Ringing Rock* as well as the Shefflex units and three of four-wheeled carriages remained the property of his executors. The absurd situation had arisen whereby if the executors had decided to withdraw this stock from the line, services would have been unable to continue.

It is thus easy to see how, purely from the point of view of rolling stock, the company was doomed so long as it failed to update. It was totally ridiculous to suppose that the line could continue indefinitely with a mixture of ageing locomotives and carriages being housed in a shed which had had half its roof blown off by a gale, and so-called economic and progressive units that gave customers such a bumpy ride that they preferred to pay a few extra pennies and travel in comfort by road. The obsession with economy was itself to contain the seeds of the company's demise.

Chapter Five

Customers and Usage

One of the most revealing ways of gauging the popularity of any railway line is by reference to its timetable. The timetables given below show how, from a tentative start, the number of trains increased greatly, so that in the immediate pre-war period the line was at its peak: after the war, however, the demand was lessened so that at the very end the number of trains had fallen off too.

1898

	a.m.	a.m.	p.m.	p.m.	Sat. only p.m.	Sunday a.m.	p.m.
Selsey	7.55	11.15	3.00	6.00	8.00	10.05	7.10
Sidlesham	8.10	11.30	3.20	6.15	8.15	10.20	7.25
Chalder	8.15	11.35	3.25	6.20	8.20	10.25	7.30
Hunston	8.20	11.40	3.30	6.25	8.25	10.30	7.35
Chichester	8.35	11.55	3.45	6.40	8.40	10.45	7.45

Return trains left Chichester at 10.15 a.m., 1.00 p.m., 4.15 p.m., 7.15 p.m. and 10.15 p.m. (Saturdays only – after arrival of the London train), and on Sundays at 10.50 a.m. and 8.00 p.m. Note that these were only the advertised station stops.

April 1910

	Mon. only a.m.	Other days a.m.	Mon. only a.m.	a.m.	a.m.	p.m.	p.m.	p.m.	p.m.	p.m.	Sundays a.m.	p.m.	p.m.
Selsey	7.00	7.40	8.30	9.18	11.30	1.25	3.05	5.50	7.05		8.50	1.20	7.00
Chichester	7.30	8.10	9.00	9.48	12.12	1.55	3.35	6.20	7.35		9.20	1.50	7.30

	Mon. only a.m.	Other days a.m.	Mon. only a.m.	a.m.	p.m.	p.m.	p.m.	p.m.	p.m.	Sundays a.m.	p.m.	p.m.
Chichester	7.45	8.38	9.15	10.35	12.48	2.20	4.25	6.32	8.00	11.20	2.00	8.15
Selsey	8.15	9.08	9.45	11.15	1.18	2.50	4.55	7.00	8.30	11.50	2.30	8.45

Note the reduced journey times, and the increased number of trains. A study of the February 1909 timetable, very similar to the above, suggests that the 9.18 a.m. 'up' would not have run on Mondays, and a Monday-only service, leaving at 9.50 a.m., ran from Selsey. A timetabler's error?

Summer 1913

	Mon. only	Other days	Mon. only	Other days	Mon. only									
	a.m.	a.m.	a.m.	a.m.	a.m.	a.m.	p.m.	p.m.	p.m.	p.m.	p.m.	p.m.	p.m.	p.m.	p.m.
Selsey	7.00	7.35	8.30	9.18	9.50	11.30	12.20	1.15	2.30	3.30	4.30	5.30	6.50	7.45	10.05
Chichester	7.25	8.05	9.00	9.48	10.18	12.00	12.50	1.45	3.00	4.00	5.00	6.00	7.20	8.15	10.35

	Mon. only	Other days	Mon. only										Thurs. only
	a.m.	a.m.	a.m.	a.m.	p.m.	p.m.	p.m.	p.m.	p.m.	p.m.	p.m.	p.m.	p.m.
Chichester	7.45	8.38	9.18	10.52	12.10	1.05	2.20	3.20	4.20	5.20	6.40	7.35	8.35	10.40
Selsey	8.15	9.08	9.45	11.22	12.40	1.35	2.50	3.50	4.50	5.50	7.08	8.05	9.05	11.10

Sunday Service

	a.m.	a.m.	p.m.	p.m.	p.m.	p.m.
Selsey	8.50	10.35	1.20	5.20	6.50	8.00
Chichester	9.20	11.05	1.50	5.50	7.20	8.30
Chichester	10.00	11.20	2.15	6.00	7.23	8.45
Selsey	10.30	11.50	2.45	6.27	7.50	9.15

Note the 6 p.m. on Sundays, speeding from Chichester to Selsey in 27 minutes, and the 7 a.m. Selsey to Chichester on Mondays, taking just 25 minutes. Journeys over 30 minutes seem to be things of the past. Note also the vast increase in afternoon trains, and the impressive Sunday service.

July 1922

Showing the time taken between station stops.

											Sundays
	a.m.	a.m.	a.m.	p.m.	p.m.	p.m.	p.m.	a.m.	p.m.	p.m.	p.m.
Selsey Town	8.15	9.55	11.50	1.25	3.05	5.55	7.20	10.35	1.40	5.30	7.10
Ferry	8.21		11.56	1.31	3.11	6.01	7.26	10.41	1.46	5.36	7.16
Sidlesham	8.25		12.00	1.35	3.15	6.05	7.30	10.45	1.50	5.40	7.20
Chalder	8.31		12.06	1.41	3.21	6.11	7.36	10.51	1.56	5.46	7.26
Hunston	8.37		12.12	1.46	3.27	6.17	7.42	10.57	2.02	5.52	7.32
Chichester	8.50	10.40	12.25	2.00	3.40	6.30	7.55	11.10	2.15	6.05	7.45

	a.m.	a.m.	p.m.	p.m.	p.m.	p.m.	p.m.	a.m.	p.m.	p.m.	p.m.
Chichester	9.05	10.55	12.40	2.20	4.20	6.40	8.25	11.25	2.20	6.20	8.10
Hunston	9.15		12.50	2.30	4.30	6.50	8.35	11.35	2.30	6.30	8.20
Chalder	9.21			2.36	4.36	6.56	8.41	11.41	2.36	6.36	8.26
Sidlesham	9.27		1.00	2.42	4.42	7.02	8.47	11.47	2.42	6.42	8.32
Ferry	9.31			2.46	4.46	7.04	8.51	11.51	2.46	6.46	8.36
Selsey Town	9.40	11.40	1.12	2.55	4.55	7.15	9.00	12.00	2.55	6.55	8.45

The obvious question which arises, of course, is why a non-stop train should take 45 minutes for the journey, and a stopping train 35 minutes!

September 1933

	a.m.	a.m.	p.m.	p.m.	p.m.	Wed. and Sat. only p.m.
Selsey Town	8.10	10.00	1.10	2.50	5.30	7.15
Selsey Bridge	8.11	10.02	1.11	2.51	5.31	7.16
Ferry	8.16	10.08	1.16	2.56	5.36	7.21
Sidlesham	8.21	10.13	1.21	3.01	5.41	7.26
Mill Pond Halt	8.23	10.15	1.23	3.03	5.43	7.28
Chalder	8.26	10.18	1.26	3.06	5.46	7.31
Hunston	8.31	10.27	1.31	3.11	5.51	7.36
Chichester	8.40	10.40	1.40	3.20	6.00	7.45

	a.m.	a.m.	p.m.	p.m.	p.m	Wed. only p.m.	Sat. only p.m.
Chichester	9.15	11.30	2.10	4.10	6.30	10.30	8.30
Hunston	9.24	11.40	2.19	4.19	6.39	10.39	8.39
Chalder	9.29	11.46	2.24	4.24	6.44	10.44	8.44
Mill Pond Halt	9.32	11.49	2.27	4.27	6.47	10.47	8.47
Sidlesham	9.34	11.55	2.29	4.29	6.49	10.49	8.49
Ferry	9.39	12.01	2.34	4.34	6.54	10.54	8.54
Selsey Bridge	9.44	12.10	2.39	4.39	6.59	10.59	8.59
Selsey Town	9.45	12.12	2.40	4.40	7.00	11.00	9.00

Note that there is by now no Sunday service; and that apart from Wednesdays and Saturdays there are just five trains a day each way, not seven as in 1922 or 11 as in 1913. Note also some of the discrepancies in journey time – nine minutes from Hunston to Chichester on the 8.31 a.m., 13 minutes on the 10.27 a.m.; five minutes from Chalder to Hunston on the 8.26 a.m., 13 minutes on the 10.18 a.m. Note that the 9.15 a.m. Chichester to Selsey took half an hour, the 11.30 a.m., 42 minutes. This, as Dr. Nichol explained in a *Railway Magazine* article, was because the steam trains, on their longer journey, took time to attach and detach wagons at intermediate points -something not done by the railbuses.

Summer 1934

	Wed. and Sat. only a.m.	a.m.	p.m.	p.m.	p.m.	p.m.	Sat. only p.m.
Selsey	8.10	10.00	1.10	2.50	5.35	7.00	9.45
Ferry	8.14	10.04	1.14	2.54	5.39	7.04	9.49
Sidlesham	8.20	10.10	1.20	3.00	5.48	7.10	9.55
Chalder	8.25	10.15	1.25	3.05	5.56	7.15	10.00
Hunston	8.30	10.20	1.30	3.10	6.03	7.20	10.05
Chichester	8.40	10.30	1.40	3.20	6.15	7.30	10.15

	a.m.	a.m.	a.m.	p.m.	p.m.	p.m	p.m.	p.m.
Chichester	9.15	11.05	11.40	2.10	4.10	6.45	7.45	10.30
Hunston	9.22	11.12	11.47	2.17	4.17	6.52	7.52	10.37
Chalder	9.27	11.17	12.00	2.22	4.22	6.59	7.57	10.42
Sidlesham	9.35	11.25	12.12	2.30	4.30	7.12	8.05	10.50
Ferry	9.37	12.27	12.16	2.32	4.32	7.16	8.07	10.52
Selsey Town	9.45	11.35	12.25	2.40	4.40	7.25	8.15	11.00

Note the slightly increased summer service but the continued absence of Sunday services.

Good connections were at one time offered to London. By catching the 4.50 p.m. train from London Bridge it was possible to reach Selsey at 7 p.m.; by catching a train leaving Selsey at 8.30 a.m. (for example on a Monday in Summer 1913) London Bridge could be reached at 10.54 a.m.; by leaving Selsey at midday London could be reached by 2.35 p.m. Card tickets in the traditional style were available when booking from various stations on Southern Region to Selsey.

Passenger usage figures are another means of charting the financial well being of the line. By the time of the outbreak of war in 1914, more than 80,000 passengers were using the line each year. In 1917, 105,169 passengers used the line, going down to 102,292 in 1919; 66,349 in 1921; 44,977 in 1923; 21,762 in 1925; 22,475 in 1927; a small rise to 22,676 in 1929; then down steeply to 13,416 in 1931; and rising to 21,088 in 1933. With passengers in 1934 paying just 8d. single from Chichester to Selsey, or 1s. return, receipts had fallen from £3,912 in 1917 to £427 in 1934. Such was the pessimism of the drivers at the end that they used to overshoot platforms, failing to spot the solitary waiting passenger on the platform until the last minute.

Records show that the line was used by many people for a large variety of reasons. Those users who are still alive at the time of writing fondly recall that they used the line for travelling to school or scouts, the lateness of the train being accepted as a watertight excuse for unpunctuality at class. Selsey was regarded by many as a pleasant destination for a day by the sea, particularly for those travelling from Chichester who would otherwise have had to change trains in order to reach Bognor. It was reported at the 1913 A.G.M., however, that in the previous year a record 89,915 passengers had used the line despite the diphtheria epidemic; that of these passengers only a small proportion were excursionists, and a larger number were now regular users of the line. The 1914 A.G.M. was able to report that 'the general working of the Company has been very satisfactory, the receipts for the year under review constituting a record, notwithstanding a heavy falling-off of passenger and other traffic during the important month of August owing to the War'. There was even talk of a new station at Selsey. The number of users rose in 1915 to 91,808.

Despite the hopes of the company that regular rather than merely casual use of the line would continue to increase, cheap day excursions were available during the summer, which allowed for a cheap day out from Selsey to the larger resorts of Worthing and Brighton. 'Restalls Excursions' offered a 3s. cheap day return from London to Selsey by train: an announcement was made c.1907 to the effect that

59. A selection of tramway tickets.

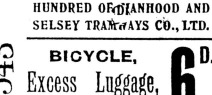

HUNDRED OF MANHOOD AND
SELSEY TRAMWAYS CO., LTD.

5543

BICYCLE,
Excess Luggage,
or DOG.

6D.

6D.

1776

HUNDRED OF MANHOOD AND
SELSEY TRAMWAYS CO., Ltd.

Saloon
SINGLE
Fare

10½ D.

2122

H.M. & S.T. Co., Ltd.

CHEAP DAY EXCURSION
SELSEY TO
CHICHESTER.
Return Fare, 9d.

C 3635

H.M. & S.T. Co., Ltd.

CHEAP DAY EXCURSION
This Half available only from
CHICHESTER to
SELSEY.
Return Fare **1/-** Third Class.

B 0159

H.M & S.T. Co., LTD.

CHICHESTER-HUNSTON
SIDLESHAM-SELSEY
CHICHESTER-SELSEY
CHILD
RETURN FARE **6d** THIRD CLASS

60 & 61. Tickets to ride the tramway.

B 0159

H.M & S.T. Co., LTD.

CHICHESTER-HUNSTON
SIDLESHAM-SELSEY
CHICHESTER-SELSEY
CHILD
RETURN FARE **6d** THIRD CLASS

4807

H.M. & S.T. Co., Ltd.

This half available only from
CHICHESTER TO
SELSEY.
Return Fare, 1/-.

'every Sunday and Thursday, cheap excursion tickets from Chichester to Selsey will be issued – on every Sunday by the 11.15 a.m. and 2 p.m. trains and on every Thursday by the 2.10 p.m. and 4.25 p.m. trains. These tickets will be available for return by any tram on the day of issue only'. Passengers, by taking the early train, could also have a long day out on the Isle of Wight. Reduced fares were seen as a special inducement to those desiring a cheap Sunday afternoon away from home. Holiday-makers coming to Selsey by train were well catered for on arrival, as a Mr. Wingham was happy to provide transport for passengers reaching the terminus at Selsey and wishing to continue to the town and the sea. Indeed he had a cartage contract with the company. In the early years of the line, the *Crown Inn* had livery stables and the coachman used to ride to meet the tram for the same reason. There was no doubt that these passengers contributed to the development of Selsey as a seaside resort.

The line also, however, conveyed a tremendous variety of freight – it was indeed thanks to the income from this, which remained reasonably steady throughout, that enabled the tramway to keep going for as long as it did. The volume was such as to justify goods trains, in which individuals were permitted to travel, subject to 'agreeing to pay the usual fare and hold the Company free from all liability regarding injury, loss, delay or inconvenience that may happen by accident to any person or property

62.   The Selsey tramway epitomised – the intimate interior of the Shefflex, an assortment of goods trucks, and not a house in sight.

whilst travelling in the said train and in joining and leaving the said train'. Some trains were actually advertised as 'mixed trains'.

The line served both the agricultural and fishing communities well, hardly surprising considering the proximity of both sea and heavily farmed land. In the early days, when Selsey Beach Station was operative, it was particularly convenient for fishermen to dispatch crabs and lobsters. The emphasis on service to farmers was shown by the propensity of the guard to walk to farms along the line to enquire if the farmer wanted the train to pick up any produce the following day – this while the guard's train waited patiently. As for fishing, the 1934 report stated that the lobster pot fishery at Selsey 'is not unimportant and most of the traffic emanating therefrom is at present conveyed by rail'. In 1933 4,464 tons of goods, 2,260 tons of minerals and 5,224 tons of coal and coke were carried by the trains. The goods were diverse in nature – milk, bricks, stone, oilcake, chaff, hay, straw, wheat, barley, oats, beercasks, grainsacks, chalk, cement, lime, manure, corn, timber and sugar (an average of 1,000 tons of beet sugar per year).

63. The tramway patrons' favourite watering-hole, together with transport home!

The line was of great value to the gasworks at Selsey, the Trojan Brickworks at Selsey (for which there was a siding) and Sadlers Mills and Oil depots at Chichester (again, sidings were provided). The company did in fact undertake to transport all classes of goods, and placed trucks procured from the main London Brighton and South Coast Railway on to the line. Ralph Selsby was one of the several carriers operating from the tramway: he was a coal merchant and contractor. International Stores was amongst a small number of firms paying for advertisement panels on the line. As well as inanimate goods, cattle, pigs and sheep were conveyed. A typical wagon in the line's later years might simply contain a young calf and milkchurns.

There were two particularly colourful users of the line. The first was the 'Italian Ice-Cream Man', Emidio Guarnacchio. He moved from Italy to England in 1905 to find prosperity, and in 1920 he and his wife, Petromilla, bought a grocery and general store in Northgate, Chichester. During his time here he started to manufacture ice-cream, and would trundle his 'Stop me and Buy one' barrow round the streets. In the summer his day would start at four o'clock in the morning when the ice-cream was made, to be sold later to thirsty holidaymakers and trippers. During the summer Emidio would travel to Selsey three days a week, using the luggage truck to transport his barrow. This continued until he was well over 70 years old.

The second was Pullinger's Mouse Trap Factory. Colin Pullinger, who advertised himself as a 'Contractor, Inventor, Fisherman, Mechanic, Paperhanger, Bellhanger, Boatbuilder, Undertaker and Clerk to the Selsey Sparrow Club', was most famous for his mousetraps. An advertisement described him as an 'enterprising elderly gentle-

64. The tramway depended to a large extent on sun-seekers for its revenue. Postcards like this must have been sent by many of its holidaying customers. This dates from 1913, when the tramway was enjoying peak popularity.

man with an inventive mind' who was very interested in his work. The mousetrap which he invented became well-known all over the country and sold in large quantities. Norman Wymer, in his book *Companion to Sussex*, asserts that the prolific production and dispatch of mousetraps from Selsey was the reason for the tramway being opened, a somewhat far-fetched observation but indicative of the importance of the mousetrap business in Selsey at the time. The trap, made from beechwood obtained from Goodwood, was described thus: 'A double compartment accessible by a round entrance in the middle through which the mouse, attracted by the bait, unsuspectingly steps upon one platform of a swinging lever bridge, so carefully poised as to descend at once, with the weight of the mouse sliding it into a smaller compartment over a wire fork, the prongs of which bar the return entrance'. The trap was all the more cruel in that mice would not die instantly but would slowly starve to death. It was, on the credit side, very easy to assemble, taking just a few minutes to construct.

An article by Bristow-Noble in the August 1932 issue of the *Sussex County Magazine* describes an encounter with Colin's son, Charles. Just as the popularity of the tram had gone into decline by this time, so had the popularity of the mousetraps: the two seemed to go hand in hand. The industry, which had been considerable, was dwindling; all that was left was one small shed and Charles Pullinger, the sole workman, who practically lived in the workshop. The 'rather wonderful' yet 'somewhat complicated' trap was, as the author pointed out, "not at all the sort which mice would have taken to without hesitation": it was self-setting, with room for more than a dozen mice who suffered no injury. The building was 'small, white, dilapidated, dingy and dusty'. The glass was covered in spider's webs, sawdust, and shavings clinging to the webs. There were hundreds of traps stocked with many more being made. Invented 70 years ago, and with a staff of 40 men and boys, it was now difficult for a visitor to know what was going on. The decline, said Mr. Pullinger Junior, could be traced to the popularity of the so-called 'penny trap'; Pullinger's cost 2s. 6d. (half a crown). He was proud that a considerable number of traps were still leaving the country, but accepted that the business was in decline – people did not want to buy them any more, and many shops had withdrawn them from sale.

In many ways the history of the tramway was similar: a flourishing beginning faded away because of failure to keep up with competition from outside, and an adherence to old-fashioned methods of working and materials.

65. A typical tramway scene – rustic with a hint of commerce.

Chapter Six

Tramway Happenings

The casual observer, if asked to pick out the two major incidents in the history of the tramway, would undoubtedly plump for the 1910 floods and the 1923 fatality. These will be described in greater detail elsewhere in this book. What the 'general' historian might fail to notice is that a number of newsworthy incidents, some more serious than others, also adorned the tramway's short life. Into this category one might put the constant 'mobile bonfires' which threatened the washing on the clothes lines in the gardens of Terminus Road, caused by the shunting of the tramway engines at the Chichester end: or the leaking firebox which emptied the tanks and caused the locomotive to be detached from the rest of the train while it puffed up to the next station for water. However, these were not 'incidents' so much as part and parcel of tramway life, and in this chapter it is proposed to examine the 'one-off' happenings which cannot be ignored in a study of the line.

Some incidents illustrate the line's quaintness. Early on in the tramway's life, the drawbridge over the canal got stuck in its upright position, unable to be lowered for several days, thus bringing all the line's traffic to a standstill. The *Chichester Observer* published a cartoon in its edition of 6 January 1909 showing an engine completely submerged in snow and a caption stating that 'the Selsey Tram got a trifle mixed up'. A few years later a happier event was deemed newsworthy, when Driver Tim Johnson who worked the line was presented with a handsome cruet by the company's staff on the occasion of his marriage. 'He is well known', the report said, 'having been with the Company for nearly twenty years.' It is reported that after the ceremony he departed with his bride, Miss Mould, for their honeymoon in Aldershot – by motor! The presentation was made by H. G. Phillips, one of the directors. A Selsey tramway conductor, Alfred Robinson, transferred to the tramway after starting his working life as a fisherman. During his two year stay on the tramway he stopped to let a woman, named Nell, on to the train and had the temerity to ask her for a date. They celebrated their golden wedding in Selsey in 1982.

Two unfortunate accidents during the war years were also worthy of mention in the press at the time. The first was in 1915, when on 14 January severe gales brought down a large elm across the track at Hoe Farm just before an 'up' train was due to pass. Fortunately the train stopped in time, and the crew were able to clear the obstruction from the line. Soon afterwards, however, a second elm blew down in the howling winds, again across the train's path, smashing a five-bar gate in the process. Fortunately a Miss Jupp of Hoe Farm witnessed this, and with great presence of mind managed to stop the train. The tree was so big that there was no question of moving it that night, thus stranding the train with the passengers unable to proceed. Miss Jupp ushered them off the train and invited them back to her house for the night. It was unfortunate, reported the *West Sussex Gazette*, that since Miss Jupp and her brother had been away, there was little in the way of supplies for the passengers' sustenance. Swift notification of the incident to headquarters, however, ensured that the line was quickly cleared. It was later reported that the winds, described in the press as a 'novel experience', had felled two of the largest trees in the vicinity, with several other trees lost. For the passengers it was a very narrow escape. Another wind-related incident loosely connected with the tramway occurred on 14 December 1929 when on the West Beach at Selsey an unoccupied bungalow, Westward Ho!, built of three carriages, blew off its supporting piers and was wrecked.

A number of accidents of varying degrees of seriousness are dotted across the tramway's history. One Monday evening in July 1917 one of the tramway passengers was a schoolgirl named Mary de Crespigny, aged about fifteen. She was going home to Selsey after Chichester High School Sports Day. Just after the tram left Hunston she was seen to fall, and the tram passed over her leg. The platelayer rushed to her assistance, as did one George Harris, a Hunston farmer, who rendered first aid by promptly binding up the injured limb to reduce bleeding. She was taken to the Royal West Sussex Hospital in Chichester where her leg was amputated below the knee.

66. A 'mishap' just below Chalder station in the late 1920s.

Despite that, the press reported her 'to be progressing favourably'! As compensation she was given a free pass on the line for life. Less serious, but significant for the person involved, was when in the late 1920s the cab of a locomotive got caught in a badly sagging 'phone line. The driver leant out and the wire struck him under the chin. What was described as a 'minor accident' at Chalder resulted in the dismissal of a platelayer, demonstrating that those in authority were sensitive to negligent acts of staff. Overshooting, alluded to in the previous chapter, had unfortunate consequences: it is said that a train overshot the platform at Chichester, ran through the buffers and finished on the pavement in Stockbridge Road. It is also reported that on 21 May 1921 the 6.15 p.m. from Chichester reached a bend 100 yards from Selsey and was derailed, causing a two-hour delay.

However, the series of accidents which gave the company most concern was that arising from confrontation between trains and road users on the crossings, where the railway met the main road. The first recorded incident took place on 29 June 1904 when a Mr. Dawson and his wife were cycling from Chichester to Selsey, unaware of the Stockbridge crossing. As they reached it they saw an engine emerging on to the road. Mr. Dawson jumped from his machine to avoid being run over. He was severely grazed: the machine received damage and Mrs. Dawson suffered shock. The *Chichester Observer* the following week reported that:

> another revolution of the wheel of a bike and the tramway crossing below Stockbridge would have been the scene of a fatal accident. The driver asserted that he whistled; but the cyclist said he had not heard the sound: the notice board was hidden by foliage and only the first line of the notice could be read.

On 22 August 1924 a motor car owned by 'Mr. Allen of Magpie Bungalow' came into collision with a tram at Ferry Crossing, smashing into the back of it and causing a derailment of the goods coach. It took some considerable time to get the tram back on the rails again.

These were by no means the only accidents, and the situation gave rise to much disquiet. The *Chichester Post* of 29 July 1929 regarded the methods employed at the crossings as 'still sadly antiquated'. It will be recalled that an objection was raised to the grant of a railway certificate under the 1864 Act because of the lack of provision of proper crossings, and the certificate was granted with the provision for gates to be erected at crossings only if the Ministry of Transport required it. The only fixed requirement appeared to be to restrict the speed of trains within a distance of 200 yards from an ungated level crossing over a public road, to 10 m.p.h. All that had actually been done, it would appear, was the erection of signs stating 'BEWARE OF THE TRAINS' (it appears that the company did not trouble to erect corresponding signs for the loco drivers, 'BEWARE OF THE CARS!'); this was coupled with the sounding of the whistle by the driver, the onus being on the engine drivers to see if the road was clear, before proceeding. The trouble was, as the *Post* pointed out, 'in these days of fast-moving cars, blowing the whistle is not enough'. Stockbridge Crossing, the paper went on to say, was obscured by a high hedge. One person who overlooked the crossing was one Dr. Hay whose car was badly damaged following a

67. Averting another accident. The *Morous* guided laboriously over the Ferry crossing, *c*.1930.

68. The perils of the ungated crossing: a Shefflex with no intervening truck passes over the main road at Ferry. Note that the bulb appears to be missing from one of the headlamps!

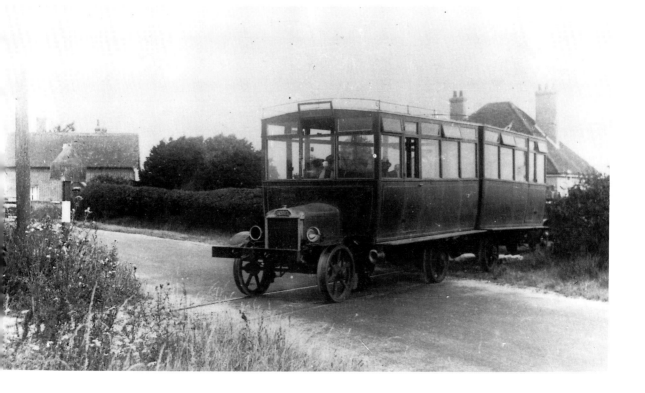

collision, although the doctor fortunately escaped injury. The driver coolly alighted and merely asked if he had heard the whistle! On 11 January 1930 the necessity for precautionary measures at level crossings was emphasised when a car driven by Mr. L. R. Snook of Festing Grove, Portsmouth, collided with the tram at Stockbridge, and was damaged: Mr. Snook was uninjured. Two days later the tram crashed into a lorry owned by Davy's of Hove, knocking it on to a private car driven by Mrs. Cover. Although there was no personal injury, the radiator and windscreen of the car were smashed.

This was the last straw. On 25 January 1930 a letter was sent to the Ministry of Transport. 'We, the undersigned, motor owners and drivers of Selsey and District have the honour to call attention to the dangerous conditions prevailing at the level crossings'. The letter went on to say that there were no complaints about the motor driven trains, only the 'light steam engines'. In the absence of gates, the letter said, the only warning was a whistle 'which can't be heard in certain conditions'. The engine, said the letter, habitually crossed the road at a dangerous speed on blind corners, leading to several accidents particularly at Stockbridge Road; although there had been no fatalities, cars had been wrecked. The letter requested an inspector

69. A collision at Stockbridge – note where the railcar is in relation to the tracks!

from the Ministry of Transport to come and see for himself and take steps to render the main road safe. The signatories, perhaps curiously, hoped that it would not be necessary to erect crossing gates, which would 'only aggravate the congestion and cause irritating delays'. A classic case, seemingly, of wanting to have one's cake and eat it! The simple solution argued the writers, was the enforcement of a rule already theoretically imposed by the management, for the train to stop, and the guard to alight and wave a red flag in the middle of the road before allowing the train to proceed. 'Providence', the writers finished in a flourish, 'cannot be tempted for too long'. The Highway Committee of Westhampnett Rural District Council went further, demanding the erection of gates at Stockbridge, Hunston and Ferry, constant attendance of employees there, maintenance by the company of the portions of road crossed, and the provision of cattle grids at Mill Pond Road. One committee member suggested that there should be gates that the driver could open himself.

Nothing happened, and providence was again tempted in 1932 when, after yet another accident at Stockbridge Road, the Ministry of Transport was at last propelled into action and one of Her Majesty's Inspecting Officers visited the scene. On arrival, he asked why the line had never been inspected before and was apparently satisfied with the explanation that it was a 'tramway' and not a 'railway'. It was proposed by the City Council that colour light signals should be provided and an estimate was obtained from Messrs. Tyers & Co., the cost being £39 10s. Of course at this stage the line was bankrupt, and ultimately it was agreed that at Stockbridge Road, Hunston (for southbound trains) and Ferry, the trains should come to a complete halt before crossing the road. A memorandum was sent to staff to that effect, also that the fireman or conductor should proceed to the centre of the road with a red signal flag by day and a red hand signal lamp by night. It is interesting that the memo ends: 'This is a renewal of the instruction issued on 9. 4. 1930'.

None of these incidents and accidents were of particular consequence in themselves. They did, however, demonstrate the vulnerability of the little line in its financial inability to prevent these accidents, as well as the line's essential quaintness.

Finally, it is worth noting that national events also touched the users of the tramway. *Selsey Billings* dated 12 May 1926 carried the following: 'When travelling to Selsey last week I was informed that for the duration of the [General] Strike the last train to leave Selsey or Chichester is now 5 o'clock. Intending travellers, please take notice'.

Chapter Seven

Humour on the Tram

This is a true story. One day the tram was making its usual, ponderous way down the line towards Selsey, and there happened to be a man on board who was in something of a hurry to reach his destination. It was thus to his intense annoyance that without warning the train pulled up in open country. 'Is this Selsey?' he demanded of the guard with presumably heavy irony. 'No', came the reply, 'there's a cow on the track'.

The cow having been forcibly evicted from the line, the tram was free to continue its journey. Having traversed a short distance in a leisurely fashion, it came to a halt yet again. Our hero with even heavier irony, called up the guard and yelled 'Another cow on the line?' The guard was emphatic. 'Confound it, no!' he retorted; and then, almost as an afterthought, 'it's the same one!' This incident so delighted Mr. Heron-Allen, one of Selsey's most distinguished historians, that he was to call to mind the words of Tennyson in *Lotus-Eaters*: 'this is the place for us; we will return no more. We will no longer roam'.

With a branch line as bizarre as the Selsey Tram, it was inevitable that humour was never going to be far away, and it was indeed the heading for this chapter that provided the headline for the *Chichester Observer*'s report of a 'Holiday Incident' which took place on August Bank Holiday 1908, and which typifies the line's character and working.

The incident would probably have never happened had it not been for the great popularity the line was enjoying at that time. Several hundred people had availed themselves of services from Chichester to Selsey for Bank Holiday sun, sea and sand, and some 400 passengers awaited the arrival of the 7.05 p.m. from Selsey back to Chichester. The platform and little waiting room were full to overflowing, while some people were lying on the grass or sitting on nearby fences. There was some speculation about how the crowds would be accommodated. Eventually the train arrived, and there was a terrific rush for seats: there was scarcely sufficient standing room, let alone seating accommodation, for even half the crowd. Eventually a cattle truck as well as the guard's van had to be requisitioned, and when the journey began, conditions were extremely uncomfortable, not helped by the continuous jolting, bumping and swaying of the train. As the *Observer* said, 'an occasional shriek told of the location of somebody's pet corn or other pedal infirmity'. To passers-by the sight of the train must have been a curious one, with passengers not only packed tightly into the carriages in sardine fashion, but sitting astride the buffers as well. Everyone seemed to be remarkably good humoured, nonetheless.

At length the train stopped at Sidlesham, where with relief one or two passengers left. It is not reported whether any passengers were waiting to join the train! It was then, and only then, discovered that in the general mêlée at Selsey, the guard had omitted to get on the train. It being apparently essential that he join the train, and there being no obvious alternative forms of transport for him to reach Sidlesham, it was necessary to send the engine back to Selsey for him. The passengers reacted incredulously when they saw the engine parting company from the train. 'They can't pull us, so they're going to push us', someone suggested. As the engine disappeared into the distance, almost 400 passengers were left stranded, four or five miles from home. The heat and discomfort of the coaches during the 20-minute wait must have been well-nigh unbearable. Except, that is, to our intrepid reporter, who stated, 'It was a good-humoured crowd, and even those who realised the probability of losing their connecting train at Chichester could not fail to appreciate the humour of the situation'. Some passengers took the opportunity to explore the surrounding countryside, while others sought the nearest hostelry, presumably the *Crab and Lobster.* The landlord must have wished such events took place more often. Speculation grew as to whether the combined efforts of the men would be able to convey the women and children home in time for breakfast – by pushing! Meanwhile some of the occupants of the cattle truck had alighted and had an opportunity of 'seeing the dainty summer dresses and pretty females who were good-naturedly suffering the inconvenience of a jumpy, jolty journey in such an inappropriate conveyance'. At last a cloud of smoke was seen, and with it the rapidly returning engine. A salvo of cheers went up as the engine puffed and snorted its way into the station. As our reporter said: 'It was a strange experience and one which will long be remembered with right good humour'.

The line's individual and quaintly rural nature was characterised by the experience of another pre-war traveller who arrived at Chichester station and, fully expecting to be directed to a side platform for his Selsey connection, asked a porter where he could get a Selsey train. 'Go down the road', he was told. 'You'll find it on the right'. It may or may not have been the same traveller who, with the short-comings of the tramway firmly fixed in his mind, decided to travel down to Selsey by bicycle in preference to 'letting the train take the strain' (or perhaps 'take the tram! no traffic jam!'). On arrival at Selsey his machine broke down, and he found himself resorting to the tram after all. Until, that is, he discovered he had no money with which to pay the fare. He had to walk home. Perhaps one should not feel excessively sorry for him (history does not recall whether he had to abandon his bicycle in Selsey and call for it at a later date), since not only did he get some exercise, but he probably stood a better chance of making it back to Chichester before the tram. With journey times of anything up to an hour for the seven and a half miles, an athlete of only average stamina could possibly compete with the tram. There are no records of runners trying to beat it, but cyclists have certainly given it a run, literally for its money. On one occasion a race did take place and apparently the only thing which prevented the cyclist from winning was the winding nature of the road, particularly round Ferry station. As for racing between the tram and the motor car (shades of Thomas the Tank Engine) the *Chichester Observer* of 12 March 1965, recalling the closure of the line 30 years before, told of the stake of £1 that was placed on the out-come of a race between a tram driver and a visitor in a racing car, from Sidlesham to Selsey. The reporter had the misfortune to be in the tram: 'Passing across the Ferry Bank the train shook so much I thought we would go into the sea, but Driver Belcher won his bet, drawing up alongside the platform as the car pulled into the yard'.

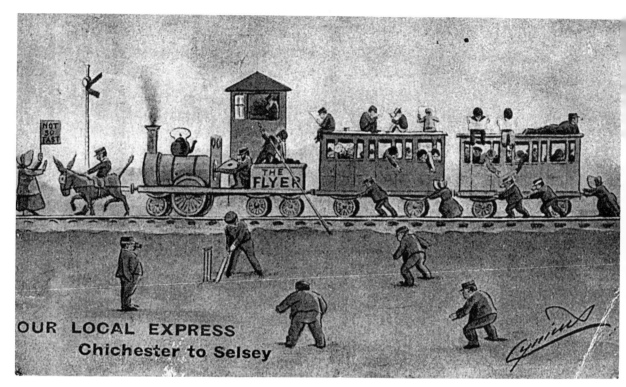

70. Cynicus' mischievous humour at work. Note the puntpole in the tender, and the kettle.

The excessively slow speeds of the trains travelling along the tramway which gave rise to the stories above had a number of causes. One of these was undoubtedly the propensity of the drivers to depart from the timetable to suit the needs, as well as the whims, of its customers and the train crews themselves. On one occasion a driver was aware that a local resident's son wished to go up to London one morning. Somewhat to his surprise, the driver reached the station where the young man was to board, and saw no sign of him. Instead of continuing his journey with a shrug, and a philosophical reflection that the next train would not be too long in coming, he jumped out of his cab, proceeded down the road to the young man's residence and knocked on his door, with a brisk 'come along, Master John, we can't wait all day for you'.

Drivers were frequently, on arriving at stations, accosted by boys who had been sent along by intending passengers to say that 'Mr. ... is not quite ready, could you wait, please?' Drivers always seemed happy to wait. Perhaps that willingness was not altogether unconnected with drivers stopping for their own needs. A Mr. Bishop recalls how a stop was made for the guard to visit a nearby farm to ask if the train was to pick up parcels or farm produce the following day! This was by no means unusual, and frequent stops would be made for journeys to nearby farms for that very purpose. Clearly it suited train personnel to make such enquiries in this way, at presumably some inconvenience to passengers. Inconvenience was an inevitable result of the frequent delays to trains caused by train crews oversleeping. This 'back-scratching' mentality, that delays were par for the course for all concerned, is exemplified in an article written shortly after the inception of the line, which recalls a tale of a driver stopping a train in order to pick some 'green stuff' for his rabbits which he had discovered growing alongside the line. On another occasion a red flag appeared before the driver. Was this red flag, suggested the writer, a signal that a turnip had been discovered at the lineside? On the contrary. It was a 'stalwart gaitered farmer who stuffed the danger signal in his pocket and calmly came aboard, doubtless thanking his lucky stars for the little railway that ran within a few feet of the garden of his house'. It is reported in 1904 that the 7.15 p.m. Selsey to Chichester train came to a standstill for over five minutes. The passengers began 'to display something akin to fear', until they were reassured by the conductor that the cause of the delay was a tobacco pouch that had been dropped onto the metals. The driver had stopped to recover it. It is also said – reflected in a cartoon of the time, showing a driver in his cab with a shotgun on his back and pheasants dangling from the rear – that one driver made a habit of stopping his train to 'bag' his Sunday lunch, while passengers alighted from the train to pick blackberries.

However, there were occasions when hold-ups occurred for reasons no less bizarre than mentioned above, which could not be attributed to frailties of drivers, guards or passengers. Straying animals have already been mentioned. Mr. Bishop's journey was enlivened by the appearance of a horse which had strayed on to the track and which the guard and fireman had to round up. Straying cows were a more regular problem. A flock of geese once settled on the line at Selsey Bridge, forcing the driver to slow to a walking pace whilst the birds, apparently unperturbed, remained obstructing the way. At Ferry, a pig strayed on to the line and was killed. It is not known whether the driver's lunch the following Sunday was roast pork. It is said that drivers kept a stock of stones for hurling at birds and other small creatures that strayed too close to the track. Another accident with a somewhat humorous twist occurred when in 1933 a collision took place at the notorious Stockbridge Road crossing (dealt with more fully elsewhere) between a locomotive and a car, forcing the car over on to its side. The lady driver got out of the car, fortunately unhurt, and proceeded to tell the driver in no uncertain terms what she thought of him. A month later there was a collision between a locomotive and a lorry. The tailboard of the lorry was forced through the windscreen of the car which pulled up behind it. The occupant was the same lady! The press wrote, 'she was highly indignant, as is only natural in the circumstances speaking very strongly to the driver about this disgraceful state of affairs'.

Although individual incidents have been picked out above, so much of what went on was humorous in nature that other incidents and reminiscences of a light-hearted nature are scattered throughout the book. There are, however, three hilarious aspects to the life of the tram which should not be overlooked – the line's nicknames, the work of Cynicus and others, and the *Selsey Tram Song*.

There can be few lines which had more nicknames applied to it. Some were descriptive and inoffensive, such as the 'Hedgerow Railway' – because the line hugged the hedgerows, the strips of land purchased being as narrow as possible for

71 & 72. More examples of Cynicus' work.

economy's sake; and the 'Blackberry Line' which could, one supposes, be applied to most country railways in the late summer. Others were less kind: 'Bumpity Bump' and 'Clickety Clack' epitomised its less than comfortable ride, while the 'Selsey Bumper' had a nice double meaning. Less subtle, and more ominous, was 'The Death Trap' – this title given to it by employees at Colonel Stephens' office!

The possibilities for exploiting this further were not lost on the cartoonist Cynicus, whose publishing company, active in the late Victorian and Edwardian periods, produced a series of postcards which added to the list of less than generous names of the line: 'The Flyer', which the line never aspired to be; and 'The Snailway Train'. Even today the picture of the giant snail pulling a packed coach ironically labelled 'Express', and the joke: 'Shall we walk, darling?'; 'We are in no hurry – let us ride' might well raise a laugh amongst hardened users of today's commuter trains.

Cynicus was not the only one to link the humble snail with the speed of the trains. In the late 1920s, a group of folk-singers composed a song especially for the line and its users, entitled *The Sidlesham Snail*:

> If you live at Sidlesham and do not keep a car,
> And you want to go to Chichester the journey isn't far:
> The journey is quite simple, the miles they are but few,
> If you leave at ten o'clock, you may get there by two.

> Chorus:
> The Sidlesham Snail, the Sidlesham Snail,
> The boiler's burst, she's off the rail.

In 1979 the East Manhood Women's Institute Group, about which more will be heard later, decided that one verse was not enough. The members, for the Autumn Group Meeting, were invited to compose a second verse for the song. The first verse was given as a guide.
The winning entry went like this:

> Selsey was the reservoir, the station was a tank:
> The people used to float into the station on a plank:
> At Sidlesham the tide came in and flooded all the bank,
> the train it tipped right over and very nearly sank.'

A copy of two entries from gallant losers is also included:

The Selsey Tram Chant

Solo: Here beginneth a section of the Railway Time Table of Nineteen Seventeen.

1. This time table is only intended to: fix the times before which the Trams will not start.

2. Unless required to pick up or set down passengers: the Trams, although scheduled to call, will not stop at all intermediate stations.

3. The Company does not undertake: that the Trams shall start or arrive.

4. At the times specified in the Table: and cannot guarantee connections with the L.B. and S.C.R. trains.

5. The insertion of the times of arrival and departure, of the L.B. and S.C.R. trains in correspondence: with the Trams of this Company.

6. Is for the convenience of the public: but the Company will not be responsible.

7. For any consequences whatever: arising from the inserted times of connections, between their Trams and the Trams of the L.B. and S.C.R.

8. Notice is hereby given: that the Company reserve the right

9. To cancel any or all of the Trams: at any time without giving further notice.

10. From the time table of Nineteen seventeen: signed: by Harry Phillips Manager.

The Sidlesham Snail

First verse as above.

2. It's fun to travel 'luggage' in the little open truck,
Jump out and pick the flowers every time the engine's stuck
And picnics can be eaten in the fields besides the track
We need to keep our strength up if we're going to journey back.

Chorus

3. Do not be despondent if you think you are too late.
Just shout out of your window, then run and jump the gate.
The Driver's very helpful and never minds a wait.
You can't expect perfection for only one and eight.

Chorus

4. Be wise and take a picnic, for altho' the trip's not long,
To faint for lack of sustenance would certainly be wrong.
And do take your umbrella – it's almost bound to rain –
As well as something good to read whilst waiting for the train.

Chorus

5. We'd rather cheer than grumble at the much maligned Snail
And her faithful crew, whose fund of humour didn't fail.
Remembering her journeys, full of laughter, joy and fun,
We shed a little tear now that her travelling days are done.

Chorus

In addition the writer cannot let the opportunity go by to supplement this collection of verse with two more of his own:

> One August day a local lass went up to town to shop:
> She got on board, but very soon, the train came to a stop:
> She heard the driver cry 'Come on!' across a nearby plot:
> Back came the answer 'Just a sec! there's tea left in the pot!'
>
> The Sidlesham Snail, ... etc.

> An athlete who did treat the little line with some disdain
> Said, I'll race the Ringing Rock to Chichester, and back again:
> But when some while later on, the train returned with pride:
> The runner was on Selsey Beach, a cool drink by his side!'
>
> The Sidlesham Snail, ... etc.

The song did not go down well with the station authorities, who threatened staff members with the sack if they were caught singing or whistling it. In 1920 it was proposed to sing the ditty at a concert in the Anchor Hall, Sidlesham. The Chichester stationmaster requested its withdrawal on the grounds that it would ridicule the line. The item was cancelled.

While it seems a little unfair to poke fun at a line into which much love, devotion, hard work and, tragically, as we shall see, a life went, it was incidents such as those described in this chapter which gave the line its individuality and, indeed, helped to inspire the love and affection in which the line was, and continues to be held.

Chapter Eight

The 1910 Floods – Harbinger of Doom?

It would not be fair to say that the 1910 floods precipitated the decline of the tram, or was in any sense responsible for its ultimate fate. Indeed it is perhaps misleading to include an account of the flood in a part of this book devoted to the line's fall. What is undeniable, though, is that it cost the tramway a great deal of money; it undermined the credibility of the tramway as an effective means of communication between Chichester and the sea; it emphasised the tramway's vulnerability to the forces of nature; and it suggested that fate was not ultimately on the tramway's side.

Before 1910 the Manhood Peninsula looked very different from how it looks today. As a result of strengthened sea defences a wide area of land between Selsey and Pagham had by 1878 been reclaimed from the sea under the Pagham Harbour Reclamation Act, leaving an area of rich alluvial mud, which provided excellent

73.   From arable land to lake in minutes, 16 December 1910. The clearing-up took longer.

farmland for growing corn and barley and grazing cattle. Effectively there was a solid, unbroken strip of coastline stretching right down the eastern side of the peninsula. The tram route crossed this area of reclaimed land between Sidlesham and Ferry.

In September 1910 Mr. Rusbridge, a Sidlesham apiarist, prophesied that the coming winter would bring some of the fiercest gales ever known in the district. It is not certain how seriously his warnings were taken or, what could have been done to avert catastrophe should his prophecy prove correct. What is certain is that, during the second week of December that year, the peninsula was gripped by a storm of unrelenting power with heavy rain and continuing gale-force south-westerlies. Finally, at 10 o'clock on the night of Thursday, 15 December 1910, the sea with an almighty roar broke through the flimsy shingle bank which had guarded the adjacent farmland for nearly 40 years. The hitherto solid line of coast was broken along a 40-yard stretch, and 2,000 acres of farmland were flooded in less than one hour. As Klapper put it: 'It [was] somewhat depressing to think of the zeal and the capital of those who drained it as alike wasted'. Between 4,000 and 5,000 acres of land were eventually submerged.

For the farmers, the floods were disastrous. For the directors, employees, and travellers on the Selsey tram, the floods were potentially calamitous, particularly in the short term. The *Chichester Observer* reported that within the hour the line, including Sidlesham station platform, was completely covered, the water rising to a height of 12 ft. There was a very real danger of damage to the permanent way. It was also Christmas: a protracted closure would rob the line of much-needed revenue from shoppers heading for Chichester. In the long-term it was clear that work would need to be done, and consequently money spent, to prevent a recurrence.

The company, to its credit, did act with considerable expedition. They advised customers that:

> owing to flooding of the Line between Sidlesham and Ferry, cheap bookings are suspended. In addition, the Company cannot book passengers through from Chichester to Selsey or vice versa. Arrangements have been made to run a bus service between Mill Pond Halt and Ferry. Every reasonable effort will be made by the Company to maintain this service but it cannot be guaranteed. Through passengers must book locally on each section of the line. The Company cannot book passengers through from Chichester to Selsey, or vice versa.

The 'bus service' spoken of was little more than a horse and cart. However, it was pressed into service remarkably quickly, the *Chichester Observer* pointing out that 'the inhabitants of the villages made their journey to Chichester just the same for their Christmas shopping, and they were merry groups which, laden with parcels of Christmas cheer, returned in the early evening by tram bus to their homes. And it was the novelty of the bus journey that seems to add to the enjoyment'.

Part of the reason for the speediness of the substitute arrangements was the good fortune that the company had in possessing locomotives at each end of the line. This enabled each locomotive to operate a shuttle, one between Chichester and Mill Pond Halt, the other between Ferry and Selsey, with the so-called 'bus' filling in the gap.

74 & 75. Scenes of devastation between Sidlesham and Mill Pond following the floods of December 1910, and efforts to get things moving again.

76. The new Selsey tramway, the famous alternative transport following the floods, December 1910.

The one thing with which the line could not cope under these arrangements was heavy goods but, as the waters receded, it was found possible to maintain a service of goods traffic along the line, running the trucks over at low tide. It is perhaps significant that whilst the company was not prepared to put its customers' lives at risk, it was prepared to chance it as far as its employees were concerned!

Work soon started in earnest in order to reopen the whole of the line to passengers. It was necessary to build an embankment two-thirds of a mile long between 12 and 15 ft. in height, and four feet above the area which the sea had reclaimed, although the floods had extended far further at the first instance. Fortunately the success of the line at the time ensured that the £2,500 cost of this work could be paid.

Following the initial trauma, the novelty of the substitute service found favour with the users of the line. It could certainly be said that this ill wind had blown a lot of good. The *Chichester Observer* of 8 February 1911 reported that the bus utilised for the conveyance of passengers was a method of transport 'which undoubtedly lends an added novelty to the journey and is appreciated by many'. That 'novelty' seemed, in the opinion of the reporter, 'to add to the enjoyment'. Indeed, the article went so far

77. Repairing the permanent way at Sidlesham.

as to suggest that the floods were themselves a potential tourist attraction – the tram giving a 'splendid opportunity to witness one of the most remarkable effects of the gale throughout the whole country'. When the stretch in question was reopened, the half-mile stretch along the embankment between Sidlesham and Ferry was to become scenically the most attractive section of the line: an example of a novelty turning into an ordinary geographical feature.

The *Observer* went on to describe a journey made by a combination of train and two-horse omnibus:

> For a couple of miles between Chalder and Ferry the Line is completely submerged and the journey to Selsey has to be made in stages by rail and bus. At Mant's, midway between Chalder and Sidlesham, the passengers have to alight and board a bus. From here they are driven through Sidlesham village a short distance beyond which the flood is encountered. It stretches right across the road and as the horses splash through, the green water is thrown up in all directions. It reaches nearly to the box of the wheel at this point and stretches along the road to a distance of 100-200 yards. The bus leans a little to the right, and the passengers are made aware of the serious effect the wash of the sea is having on the road. From the top of the bus one has a clear view of the

78 & 79.   The results of the labours – the Selsey tramway is raised on to the new embankment at Sidlesham, 1911.

surrounding countryside. A few hundred yards away the tops of the telegraph poles at regular intervals denote the spot where the Selsey Tram Line lay submerged in eight, ten or even twelve feet of water. At Ferry the train is again boarded. It is fortunate that the Line is prepared for emergencies and had their rolling stock divided between Chichester and Selsey. Although the Line is here clear of water there is still a wide expanse stretching on either side. With the light railway under water for practically 2 miles its only possible communication with the outside world is by the half flooded road and this will have to be raised and strengthened if it is not to be washed away.

Following the closure of the line in 1935, Harriet James wrote a letter to the *West Sussex Gazette* and recalled the 1910 floods. To her, as to so many people, the engines themselves had personalities: she fondly recalled one engine and some coaches remaining 'smugly at their home address', busily plying between Ferry and Selsey; another engine, 'resident at Chichester' conducted its business between there and Mill Pond Halt; whilst the omnibus in the middle 'wended its way' from Selsey to Ferry each day to commence the shuttle. Mrs. James recalled how, despite the existence of a tram along that section of the route, she sometimes persuaded the genial bus driver to let her travel all the way by bus, even though it was not strictly permitted. At Ferry passengers left the tram, changing 'into or on to' the omnibus. As she says, 'with a crack of the driver's whip we were off, at a dignified pace, over the road to Sidlesham, and beyond to Mill Pond Halt. Athletic and energetic schoolboys ran behind it'. 'Progress', she says, 'was somewhat regal: effectively, a coach and pair with outrunners! At Mill Pond Halt, the all-change sounded again, and passengers disembarked in readiness for the Chichester train.' The engine was supposed to be waiting but often it was not there. On fine mornings, Mrs. James explained, this was not a problem: there might be time for a stroll in the nearby lanes and fields, picking wild flowers or 'generally vegetating'. 'As long', she says, 'as we kept an alert ear for the engine's shrill whistle of triumph on arriving, or for the noisy rumble of the advancing train, one could always rush back in time to mount it before its retreat to Chichester. When the train chugged slowly into Chichester, the morning was often well advanced and school had assembled long since.' It was, as she said, always a legitimate excuse for being late, and was accepted with a smile.

Mrs. James' reference to passengers clambering 'into or onto' the omnibus recalls the practice of some passengers of sitting on top of the coach rather than inside. The reason was to avoid getting wet when the bus passed through the floods and covered the floor of the coach with water. One is left to speculate what option was exercised when it was raining!

It was perhaps fortunate that no train was running through the affected area at the time of the flooding so there were no fatalities. Remarkably, too the permanent way remained undamaged and the line reopened soon afterwards, apparently in June, in time for the following summer's holiday traffic. The 1913 A.G.M. of the company was pleased to report how well the new embankment had stood up to further storms and extraordinarily high tides early in the year. Morale was still high: the Light Railway Order was being applied for, and the floods were, as far as everybody could tell, merely a temporary setback which would soon be forgotten. Indeed, despite other weather-related incidents, reported earlier in the book, the embankment was to

80.   Sidlesham Mill from the tramway after the floods, ironically in the last stages of decay following the land reclamation over 30 years before. It was demolished a few years later.

protect the Selsey Tram from any further major flooding for the remainder of its existence.

Nonetheless, the flood had happened. Whilst it had novelty value for tramway passengers, and was a source of enjoyment for children, it wreaked havoc upon Selsey and the surrounding area and cost the tramway company, as has been said, a lot of money, with no guarantee that there would not be a repetition in years to come. It was a chilling reminder that the line's future security could not be assured: a reminder which was to be reinforced by the line's major tragedy just 13 years later.

Chapter Nine

Fatal Accident

For the train crew and passengers, Monday 3 September 1923 was just another Monday morning. The first train of the day was ready to leave Selsey – the second *Chichester*, otherwise known as *Wembley* with a consignment of 20 passengers and goods. At 8.15 a.m., with Mr. Stewart driving and Mr. Barnes (known as 'Dirg'), the fireman, it left, confidently proceeding northwards towards the historic cathedral city. The start of a new working week: an ordinary working day.

The events that immediately followed, however, were anything but ordinary. The first indication that something was badly wrong was a series of violent bumps which threw passengers from their seats, just after the train had passed Golf Links Halt. A split second later the *Wembley* had jumped the rails and careered down the embankment to rest in the marshes beneath. The presence of the marsh was to save many lives: it checked the progress of the locomotive, and the three coaches, although totally removed from the rails, remained upright.

Mr. Rusbridge was first on the scene, and he lost no time in telephoning the rescue services. When they arrived, they found that the buffer of the first coach had burst through the engine's coalbunker, and as a result Mr. Barnes, the fireman, was crushed against the boiler. Mr. Stewart had escaped with scalds; none of the passengers were injured.

The rescue attempt was severely hampered by the escape of steam. It was necessary to saw through the left-hand buffer of the first carriage. It was not until one o'clock, some four and a half hours after the accident, that the rescuers managed to clear sufficient wreckage to get to Barnes' body, and when they did so, they found it was too late. The Hundred of Manhood and Selsey Tramway had claimed its first life. The press, two days later, in describing the 'shocking accident', spoke highly of the work of the company's officials in attempting to effect the rescue especially with the risk of explosion and the constant presence of steam. They congratulated the rescuers 'in not desisting from their efforts until they had made sure the poor fellow was past human aid'. This would have been of little consolation to Mr. Barnes' relatives!

Traffic on the line was suspended for two days, but of far greater concern to the tramway company was the inquest which followed. The company realised that a finding of negligence on their part would not only reflect badly upon them in the community, but also that the resultant undermining of public confidence would cause even more business to be lost to the roads. It would also serve as a painful reminder of the amount of money which might need to be spent by them to ensure the safety of future passengers on the line.

The inquest was to last four hours. A coroner presided and a jury was empanelled. The hearing was to be a damning indictment on the maintenance and upkeep of

81 & 82. The tramway's blackest day, 3 September 1923. Fretful passengers, worried officials and bent rails after *Chichester II* took the plunge.

the tramway, and the greatest possible blow to its morale.

The coroner having begun by reminding the jury that they would need to trace negligence directly to some individual, Charles Stewart, the driver, gave evidence first. He confirmed that he had left Selsey with the train at 8.15 a.m. and the engine had been in good order. Things had begun satisfactorily, until 300 yards short of where the accident took place when the steam was shut off. It was still off when the rails were jumped. He tried to brake, but to no effect. Stewart was pinned in the right-hand side of the cab. He found the deceased crushed against the centre of the boiler by the buffer of the first coach. Stewart himself received a slight scald. He tried to get Barnes out but he was too tightly wedged. He maintained that the impact had killed Barnes at once.

> Coroner: What speed were you travelling?
> Stewart: 16 miles per hour.
> Coroner: Was that usual?
> Stewart: Yes.
> Coroner: Who employed you?
> Stewart: Mr. Stephens.
> Coroner: Did he warn you?
> Stewart: No.
> Coroner: Would you agree that the Line is not in a very satisfactory condition?
> Stewart: We have always taken great care in coming along it.
> Coroner: What caused it?
> Stewart: I've examined the spot. It looks as though the rails spread out, and the engine dropped between them.
> Coroner: What about the sleepers?
> Stewart: They were not in a bad condition on the whole. One or two might have been bad.
> Coroner: Was the Line examined daily?
> Stewart: Yes.
> Coroner: That day?
> Stewart: Yes.
> Coroner: By whom?
> Stewart: Symes, the foreman platelayer. Three weeks ago I spoke about a bad joint to Symes. I found it bumpy. Symes said he would attend to it. He told me he'd put a gauge on and found it to be all right. I was satisfied. The foreman asked if I noticed any bump after this joint had been examined and I replied that I felt an occasional bump.
> Jury: Are employees in the habit of making complaints to each other instead of to a responsible official?
> Stewart: If we felt anything was wrong we spoke to the platelayer.

The next person in the witness box was William Walker, the guard. He told the inquest that he was issuing tickets at the time and felt a bumping. He went to see if any passenger was hurt and found none, then he went to the engine and saw what had happened, subsequently discovering Barnes dead. Walker told the inquest he had been a guard for 20 years. There was a handbrake at the rear of the train which he could control, but even if it was possible to manipulate – which was doubtful – the operation of it would not have prevented what happened.

Coroner: Where did you get your work instruction from?
Walker: The Selsey office.
Coroner: Did you have cause to complain about the Line to anyone?
Walker: No, the train has come off once before, about two years ago.
Coroner: What do you think of the Line?
Walker: It's not my business to say.
Coroner: Do you think it's been sound enough?
Walker: I've travelled the Line for twenty years and it's as good as when I first travelled. The foreman ganger has walked the Line every morning.
Coroner: Can you express an opinion as to the cause?
Walker: No.
Coroner: That's funny.

The next witness was Foreman Platelayer Symes. He told the inquest he had been foreman platelayer since 15 August, and had been instructed to examine the line each morning. He told the inquest he had been a platelayer with the Great Western Railway for 20 years, and had noticed nothing wrong with the piece of line in question; neither had he any complaints about it. The spot the driver had alluded to in his evidence was a quarter of a mile away. The driver was recalled and confirmed that he had complained about the line at the spot where the accident took place.

Coroner: Were the sleepers good or bad?
Symes: I can't say they were good, I have seen worse ones.
Coroner: Had they become soft and rotten?
Symes: No, sir.
Coroner: Did you report these sleepers on that spot?
Symes: I did elsewhere. I restored eighteen a day.
Coroner: Why didn't you report that these sleepers were bad?
Symes: I didn't think they were bad enough to be reported just yet. The accident was in no way due to the rails. The engine jumped them.
Coroner: You give me the impression of trying to cover something up.
Symes: I didn't see the marks of the wheels of the engine inside the rails. The sleepers are up on the track now. If anything is burnt this is not known to me.
Coroner: Do you consider the sleepers now throughout the Line are in satisfactory condition?
Symes: No, but there are good sleepers in places. We're putting new ones in.
Jury: What is your tour of duty?
Symes: My duty is to walk from Chalder to Selsey each morning starting at six. The rest is covered by another man.
Jury: Would you be surprised to learn that two hundred yards away from the scene, a sleeper could be lifted out?
Symes: Okay – some might not be fastened tightly. Whenever one is found that is loose – it is knocked in.
Jury: The position of the right rail suggests the driver is right.
Symes: I can't answer. I felt the Line was safe and if I thought anything was the matter I would have reported it .....

Dr. Humphrys said that Barnes must have been killed at once. His body was in a terrible state with a severe blow to the heart. He also had bad scalds, and an implement in the cab had pierced through his back.

83. A close-up of *Chichester II* after the accident. It is remarkable that the engine was able later to return to normal running.

Colonel Stephens was next to be called. He certified that he had been a Lieutenant Colonel in the Royal Engineers Reserves and he deeply regretted what had happened. He was responsible for 12 different lines and had to delegate his duties to assistants. He had not been down for about eighteen months. He said that between 1920 and 1923, 4,000 sleepers had been sent down to the line – secondhand sleepers. The engine was of recent origin. He suggested that the accident had been caused by an invisible obstruction of some kind. Mr Phillips, the manager, then gave evidence. He had instructed Symes to forward weekly reports in writing, and report any emergency. He had never received any report concerning the piece of line where the fatality occurred. Drivers were instructed not to exceed 12 miles per hour and also to reduce speed at curves. He had found Symes an efficient employee.

Finally P.C. Pope was called, and he gave perhaps the most crucial and telling evidence of all. He certified that he had found rails lying on their sides, and loose nails, and he had found indications of rails having been turned over. He had not, in the vicinity of the accident, seen one sleeper that was completely sound: there was always one rotting in one part or another. Two bolts were missing, having been torn out by the engine; others were so loose they could be lifted out.

The jury thus had to assess a number of different stories: the driver, who seemed reluctant to shift any of the blame on to the platelayer or indeed on to the general condition of the line; the guard, who refused to commit himself; the platelayer, who denied that there was anything wrong with the line's condition; Colonel Stephens, who put the accident down to an invisible obstruction; Mr. Phillips, who implied that his platelayer's denials were to be accepted; and P.C. Pope, who laid the blame at the door of those responsible for the maintenance of the rails and the sleepers.

84. Scene of devastation 70 years later: the embankment by the golf links as it appears now.

The final verdict was one of accidental death, but the chief engineer of the company was held indirectly to blame as there was evidence of neglect in the track's upkeep. The *Daily Chronicle's* headline, 'RAILWAY LINE IN ROTTEN STATE – COMPANY CRITICISED AT INQUEST', did precious little to enhance the standing of the company or its officials. Colonel Stephens' 'shoestring' railway had led to a tragic but avoidable death.

The Selsey Parish Council, clearly dissatisfied with this outcome, demanded a public inquiry. The Ministry of Transport, however, had other ideas. A Mr. E. W. Rowntree, in reply, wrote:

> With reference to your letter of 17th September 1923 concerning the accident that occurred on 3rd September to a fireman named Barnes when a tram became derailed at the Hundred of Manhood and Selsey Tramway: I am directed by the Minister of Transport to state that the undertaking in question is not authorised by statute and the Minister has no power to hold an inquiry into the causes of the accident. As you are aware, however, an inquiry into the cause of death of the fireman was held by the coroner and the jury expressed the opinion that there was evidence of neglect in the upkeep of the line.

There lay the final paradox – the fact that the line was – strictly speaking, illegal, prevented the matter going any further. How much more a public inquiry would have achieved is open to debate. It might, in the last resort, have led to closure. As it was, the line was to continue for another 12 years, having ironically gained legality a year later. But the damage had been done. The fatality, the short-term disruption, the refusal to accept responsibility, and the loss of credibility, was to hasten the decline of the line's fortunes. As Barnes died, so the tramway began to die with him.

Chapter Ten

Downfall of the Selsey Tram

The 1915 A.G.M. of the tramway company described the year just gone as a 'remarkably good year'. It was pointed out, however, that to take advantage of Selsey's so-called 'gold mine' the company must have 'proper machinery and a proper line'. It seemed a 'grievous pity' that shareholders 'did not take their courage in both hands and do something to enable them to make the line worthy of the service which it was expected to provide'. Mr. Edward Heron-Allen, at the following year's A.G.M. also sounded a warning note about the 'apathy of the shareholders'.

These words were to prove more than a little significant. In many ways it could be said that the tramway company had never had it so good in 1915. It had the go-ahead for reconstruction of the permanent way and the extension to the Witterings; it had seemingly put behind it the 1910 floods and taken remedial measures to ensure that there was no repetition; and passenger traffic was at its highest ever level. With its fleet of locomotives serving the people of Selsey, and the prospect of providing economical and reliable transport right across the Manhood, there was undoubtedly the potential to turn the tramway into a highly profitable, successful and lasting concern.

Yet, less than 20 years later, some of those who attended the A.G.M. would be witnessing a scene of desertion and dereliction along the eight-mile stretch of line which had carried the tramway, as this noble little concern collapsed in ruins. What was it that caused a flourishing enterprise with great potential to disappear almost without trace in such a short space of time? The answer was, quite simply, an irreversible and unremitting exodus of traffic, both travellers and freight, to the roads.

With the standing that the tramway had built up in the community, and the dedication of so many to its cause, one might have wondered why the company was unable to prevent the drift from iron to concrete. A number of the answers will have been self-evident from earlier chapters – the refusal to purchase or commission new and comfortable rolling stock, inability to maintain the track and existing stock to anything like acceptable levels, the bad memories of the 1910 floods and, much worse, the 1923 fatality and the lapse of the order enabling the Wittering extension to go ahead. This last problem was no doubt an effect of the war and the shareholders' apathy. These factors would, in due course, be coupled with an unprecedented and similarly irreversible ascendancy of the internal combustion engine.

The First World War saw a dramatic increase in the use of sophisticated technology. Some of this was transferred to civilian life and one of its effects was to accelerate the development, and improvement in reliability, of the internal combustion engine. Cars began to pour out of the factories at a hitherto unheard-of rate. Selsey acquired its first motorised taxi service, courtesy of H. J. Blake, during the 1920s, and Fidler's Carrier service, really no competition for the tram until the end of the war, became motorised. In a seven-day period in August 1923, 3,840 motorcars were seen coming out of Selsey. On 8 August 1926, 275 cars entered Selsey between 10.45 a.m. and 4.00 p.m.; 335 on 29 August. Clearly the flexibility, ease and comfort of car travel was preferable to the strait-jacketing and discomfort of rail travel, a fact reflected right across 20th-century British transport history.

The concurrent rise in popularity of the motorbus at the expense of the tram perhaps merits more explanation. It is an amazing fact, but a fact nonetheless, that in 1978 Southdown buses plying the Chichester-Selsey route were still not bettering the best speeds achieved on the railway! The journey time of 45 minutes advertised when a regular bus service started between the two locations in July 1920 compared unfavourably with the 35-40 minute average journey time managed on the tramway. The bus fare, too, was more than the train fare: 8d. to go on the train, 11d. on the bus! Yet, notwithstanding these factors, hitherto loyal supporters of the tramway began to prefer the bus. Flexibility was a major factor: buses could make any number of stops en route, providing almost a door-to-door service if necessary, whereas rail passengers could have a long journey from the nearest station to their home. Comfort was another: passengers, drawn to the buses by the sheer novelty value, found themselves obtaining a smoother ride. The buses were more reliable than the

85. Competition for the tramway – a Southdown bus coping quite adequately with the flooding, 1931.

trains: a Mr. Dick Allen recalls watching the tram 'in the distance, chugging along', whilst the bus on which he was travelling 'sped past it'. Most ironic, however, was the fact that it was actually a great deal easier for passengers passing through Chichester on their way to Selsey, to use the bus. For some reason it was extremely difficult to arrange a 'through booking' to Selsey by rail from a station not on the tramway. A passenger travelling to Selsey from, for instance, London, would almost certainly arrive at Chichester without having financed his journey to Selsey. Faced with a 150-yard walk to the tramway station, laden with heavy luggage, and the likelihood of a considerable wait for a Selsey-bound train, most passengers tended to opt for buses which not only pulled up right outside the mainline station but provided much better connections with mainline trains, both arriving at and departing from Chichester. It is significant that the bulk of the traffic between the terminal points – 19,363 of 21,088 passengers in 1933 – originated on the line, suggesting that through traffic by then was almost non-existent.

As the press at the time said, 'the Company invented all kinds of reasons why people should patronise their Line but they looked at their rolling stock and track and said "No, for pleasure we prefer other means". A joyride upon the Selsey Tramline was not within the scope of most people's predilections'. John Scott-Morgan baldly stated: 'As the Tramway was noted for being very slow, people quickly changed their mode of transport when buses appeared on the scene'. Baker, in his *Sussex Villages*, was even more blunt, describing the tramway as being 'done to death by the motorcar and the Southdown bus'. Dr. Hugh Nichol, an enthusiast of the tramway, had to admit that 'little if any inconvenience will result from closure – bus facilities have for long satisfied public needs'.

Klapper in his 1932 *Railways in Sussex* series made a last impassioned plea for travellers to return to the railway, stating how the railways were assisting the coal industry, whilst road transport operators 'bolster up the finances of the foreign petrol magnates'. He went on: 'preference for rail travel may be considered an even more practical way of assisting our distressed coal and steel areas than any that have been discussed in the daily press of recent months'. But like, it seems, those of the environmentalists of our own day, Klapper's pleas came too late. Passenger traffic plummeted, as can be seen from figures quoted earlier in this book, and receipts plummeted with it. A typical day in April 1934 might see 11 passengers get on at Hunston, 13 at Sidlesham, or 18 at Selsey.

On 31 March 1931 the company defaulted on payment of interest due on 'B' debentures, having failed to effect redemption of those due for repayment. The debenture holders issued writs for enforcement of payment of overdue interest and redemption. A second writ was issued by Colonel Stephens who had a controlling interest in the company – claiming, as a holder of 'A' debentures, to enforce payment of monies, and calling for the appointment of a receiver. Although Mr. Heron-Allen and other holders of 'B' debentures opposed this, a receiver was appointed on 8 May. £7,000 in 'A' debentures and £5,000 in 'B' debentures were owing, and there was a mortgage of £1,000. Against this was the entire rolling stock and 'other working property', consisting of a large plot of freehold land fronting on to Stockbridge Road, eight miles of freehold line with stations, water tanks and associated property, a row of houses in Station Road and a considerable amount of traffic in goods, coals, building materials and other commodities.

As the receivership took effect, two lifelines were offered to the company. The first was the acquisition of a plot of land at Hunston by a sugar refinery in 1933. Government aid was promised for the erection of a new refinery which would have provided considerable traffic of freight as well, possibly, as employees. The railway was ideally positioned to meet that need, and the benefits to it would have been great. Sadly, however, the subsidy was guaranteed for a year only and it was felt that the outlay was unjustified.

86. For avoidance of doubt – the closure becomes public knowledge, 1935.

The second was the hope that the Southern Railway would be prepared to purchase the line. The Southern Railway had come into existence in 1922 in the so-called 'regrouping' under which a vast number of private railway companies had come under the auspices of one administrative body. Later, of course, this was to become the southern region of British Rail on nationalisation in 1948. Once the tramway became bankrupt, the intervention of Southern Railway seemed the only guarantee of long term survival. The *Chichester Post* was optimistic: it would be worthwhile, the reporter said, for Southern Railway to acquire it at a price which would satisfy the creditors' claims. It would be a remunerative asset to Southern Railway, with great potential for goods and passenger traffic. 'It may therefore be confidently asserted', the report went on in ringing tones, 'that a new era has dawned for Selsey and increased prosperity may be anticipated when the improved facilities for communication with the outer world are considered.' (Presumably it was anticipated that a proper link line with Chichester mainline station would be built.) It was thus that a feasibility study was carried out. In 1934 the report was produced, highlighting many of the difficulties besetting the tramway. The major difficulties were as follows:
(i) Legality. The report reiterated that operations had commenced in 1897 without legal status, and mentioned the failure of the management fully to implement the terms of the 1924 Railway Certificate before its expiry, particularly with regard to the takeover of the tramway company by the railway company which brought into question exactly what effect the certificate had really had.

(ii) Finance. The report pointed out that in 1899 an increase of share capital from £12,000 to £16,800 was authorised but £2,400 remained unissued: between 1911 and 1924, £5,000 of debentures were issued and these became impossible to redeem. Fares were fixed too low, the cheap day return from Chichester to Selsey for instance was a shilling. Possibly, the report stated, 1s. 3d. would be charged by the Southern Railway. Some usage of the company's property was not even charged!

(iii) Topography. The line, the report stated, had to be constructed to conform with the strips that had been acquired by treaty and possibly the best layout for a railway from Chichester to Selsey was not obtained.

(iv) Equipment. Although the rails bore around 42 lbs. to the yard initially, the report found that many of these were still in use, with it being unlikely that they would only go 36 lbs. to the yard: the maintenance standard was poor. Axle loads exceeding 10 tons on the line were now unacceptable. No fixed signals were provided and the points were insecurely fixed. 'Presumably', the report said, 'if the West Sussex certificate were in force and the line inspected by the Ministry this requirement would have to be met'. Of course there had never been such an inspection. Accommodation gates were described as being 'in disrepair'. Fencing 'needs strengthening'; the halts were described as 'elementary timber structures' and the rolling stock 'little value beyond scrap' with one of its three locos 'beyond

87.   The site of Selsey Bridge station, photographed in 1947.

88. Chichester station with hoarding, after its closure in the late 1930s. Advertising provided a source of revenue for the tramway. Note the gas-works in the background, long since pulled down.

repair', two carriages in 'hopeless condition', one in 'bad condition', a rail motor in 'poor condition', and a third of the stock was on loan anyway from the executors of Colonel Stephens!

(v) Working. The report cited the unsatisfactory situation concerning the crossings of main roads, particularly the agreement that trains should have to come to a halt at certain crossings and that the £39 10s. 0d. required to erect colour light signals was beyond the financial reach of the company. Further, the curves and gradients on the line reduced its maximum speed still further. The report noted that the line possessed no goods brake van at all. Connections with London were 'in a number of cases not satisfactory' with no Sunday service. The average speed of the rail motors, being 14.7 m.p.h., and mixed trains 10 m.p.h., was described as 'low', the trains 'not infrequently late'.

(vi) Customers. It was remarked that although a number of traders were served from the property of the tramway at Chichester, the traffic, except for passing the exchange points and being shunted into position by the tram engine, did not go down the Selsey line at all. The passenger fall-off was 'of course, largely attributable to road competition' with hourly departures of buses throughout the day with double deck buses employed and thus about 750 passenger seats offered each way daily, Sundays included, between Chichester and Selsey. Bus competition was described as 'disastrous' to the tramway company because of its better frequency and connections, its proximity to Southern Railway and its running via the main roads and hence the centres of Hunston, Sidlesham and Selsey.

The conclusion was inevitable: 'there is no doubt that the resuscitation of the Line will involve substantial expenditure being incurred. The track must be brought into a condition to allow the Line being worked at speeds which will enable it to compete with the bus service'. This would have meant the provision of an 'up to date railcar with good acceleration and braking power' with either bridges, fully manned crossings or colour light signals; the track brought into a good state of repair; 40 m.p.h. speeds; and an hourly service. However, any railcar could contain only very limited luggage accommodation.

The report demonstrated just how desperate the tramway's plight had become. Creditors were piling up – debenture interest of over £5,274, the executors of Colonel Stephens being owed £7,467 13s. 7d., the Southern Railway being owed nearly £2,000, the Inland Revenue over £300. Usage even on August Saturdays, traditionally the busiest time of the year for holidaymakers, was sparse, with no passengers carried at all on the 11.40 a.m. train from Chichester to Selsey on 12 August 1933 and just two on the 8.10 a.m. from Selsey to Chichester the same day. The enormity of the prospective commitment and the tremendous difficulty in engaging in realistic competition with the buses was enough to convince Southern Railway that the Selsey Tramway should not become part of its network. The negotiations between the company and Southern Railway broke down irretrievably late in 1934, and this coincided with the reduction of the service to just one train on weekdays, leaving Selsey at 10 a.m. and getting to Chichester at 11 a.m., leaving Chichester at 11.30 a.m. and arriving in Selsey at 12.15 p.m. The head had been placed on the block and it was only a matter of time before the axe fell.

The *Weekly News* of 15 December 1934 wrote an article about the tramway in its death-throes which started, 'See Naples and Die? Why Naples? Why not go to Selsey and go by train? You will never regret it.' The writer arrived at Chichester 'all agog' to go to Selsey but found 'alas, no train'. The one train had already gone, and the writer had to travel to Selsey by car. There he saw two or three veteran coaches, 'rather sad and sorry', no longer in service. 'It was at the station itself that we saw the tram. Imagine two old Ford motor-coaches built up on railway wheels and coupled at the back ... looked so funny. One of the station employees didn't see anything funny in it. I suppose when one is accustomed to such a train it ceases to be funny.' He describes a man in a peaked cap jumping down, cranking the engine. 'A little man in a bowler hat gazed at the goods train and said "Well, I suppose you'd better get along", which it did, with a roar and spluttering.'

The end came on Saturday 19 January 1935. The 12 staff, from superintendent to messenger boy, were paid off, and the line was put up for sale by tender. Some of the property in the company's custody was now the property of Colonel Stephens' executors and by the time this or the proceeds had been returned to them, it was clear that the final proceeds of sale would not be nearly enough to satisfy the demands of the mortgagees and debenture holders. It was sold on 3 March 1936 to a

Mr. F. Watkins of Sling, in Gloucestershire, for the princely sum of £3,610. When one remembered the capital outlay in 1897, it was by anyone's reckoning a pathetic figure. The Hundred of Manhood and Selsey Tramway Company was struck off the register of companies on 23 September 1938.

The Selsey Tramway, by virtue of its closure, attracted a *Daily Express* reporter

89. Old station signboards have their uses. This picture dates from 1935.

and resulted in a feature article on the Monday following closure: all the observations made there have been reproduced in the appropriate parts of this book. The eulogising was left to the local press, especially the *Chichester Post*. In its first article it wrote: 'Unwept, unhonoured and unsung, the Hundred of Manhood and Selsey Tramway, rechristened in its decrepit old age the West Sussex Light Railway passes out of existence, crushed by the Juggernaut of progress after being etiolated by the paralysis of neglect. Those who have watched it staggering to its inglorious end will neither be saddened nor surprised'. Its second article remarked:

> puffing, bumping Selsey Billy is no more. He has served his purpose and, like the old horses he superseded, he has become worn out and out of date. Although abused as a one horse affair [it had] a most extraordinary virility. During the last few years Billy has been the subject of many a quip in Chichester – it must be admitted that he has made his contribution to the history of this corner of West Sussex. Not only did he establish a newer, quicker, more regular means of communication – he opened up the rich agricultural land between Chichester and the Bill. As the years wore on, Billy wore with them. Now the Line is closed. People are already talking of a successor – an ordinary gauge track with fast engines. We shall soon know if this is true or not.

Unfortunately there was no truth in this. The line was gradually – although not immediately – dismantled, and the station buildings, such as they were, came down too. Chichester station was demolished and absorbed into the British Rail goods yard. Selsey Town station was dismantled by German P.O.W.s in 1946 and the yard

AT HUNSTON STATION.

16   Two iron water tanks, each 4ft. by 4ft. by 4ft. 6ins., with timber framing and galvanized water barrel and part of water pump

17   About 32 yards of timber lattice fencing and sign board

18   The galvanized iron and timber station building, lined matchboarding, in 2 compartments, fitted cupboard, shelves and seats, with canopy. Size 20ft. by 9ft. 9ins.

19   The Stafford blue brick platform coping, about 40 yards run

20   Twenty-five sleepers (grade 3)

21   Fifty ditto (ditto ½-round)

22

23

AT CHALDER STATION.

24   About 33 yards of timber lattice fencing and sign board

25   The Staffordshire blue brick platform coping, about 38 yards

26   The corrugated iron and timber station building of 2 compartments, lined matchboarding, with canopy fitted cupboards and seats, about 20ft. by 9ft. 9ins.

27

AT MILL POND HALT.

28   The timber platform staging and supports, about 16yds. by 2yds, 7 sleepers and the timber rail fencing

29   Timber-built span roof shed about 7ft. 6ins. by 4ft. and a 9ft. iron frame platform seat

30

90 & 91. A schedule of some of the tramway items for sale following closure.

AT SELSEY STATION.

181   Corrugated iron and timber Station building, comprising General and Ladies' Waiting Rooms, with W.C., and inner and outer offices, lined matchboarding with canopy and fitted fireplace, range of cupboards and shelves and seats ; size 42ft. by 16ft. and the lean-to corrugated store shed and urinal adjoining

Contents of above :—

182   Mahogany extending table with 2 extra leaves, 5ft. 9ins. by 5ft. 9ins.

183   Small deal kitchen table, and a wall mirror plate, 10ins. by 36ins.

184   Two birch office chairs

185   Two ditto

186   Painted nest of 5 drawers with cupboard under, 3ft. 3ins. wide

187   Painted nest of 6 drawers, 2ft. 3ins. wide

188   4ft. oak roll-top desk, fitted 8 drawers

189   Iron letter press and stand, 4 stationery racks and 6 letter baskets

190   Iron fireproof safe by *G. Withers*, 22ins. by 24ins. by 30ins.

191   Linoleum as laid, spark guard, iron kerb and sundries

192   Quantity of sundries

193   Salters' 56lb. spring balance

used for coal storage. With the dismantling of the station, which had been used as a sports pavilion, much of the official railway documentation was destroyed. In 1963 the station platform could still be seen by the side of the coal yard. Sidlesham station fared better, being re-erected in 1948 in North Mundham. Incidentally, the *Island Cottage Inn* at North Mundham acquired its own tramway souvenir, a third-class ticket for a single journey between Chichester and Selsey, which formed part of the decoration of the lampshade over the bar billiards table!

Beacon House, where the line's opening celebration banquet was held, has long since been washed away by the sea. The absence of conventional signalling and other railway landmarks such as bridges meant that it did not take long for evidence of the line's existence to be almost completely smothered, although it is fair to say that the track could be walked with ease for some years after closure. The one overbridge on the line, near Selsey, was eventually filled in and gradually flattened. A later chapter will relate what evidence of the line remains today: suffice it to say that those who purchased the land from Mr. Watkins found more profitable use for it than running railway engines.

What better epitaph could this little line have than this moving commentary: 'With a last, pathetic spectacle of one of its engines lingering for a time in rusty decrepitude with grass and weeds sprouting on cab and side tanks, the Company passed into local history. It created few artefacts but it left a legacy of admiration and nostalgic smiles'.

Chapter Eleven

The Tramway in Modern Times

On 19 January 1935, the Selsey Tram died. No longer would trains ply the eight-mile stretch between Chichester and the tip of the Manhood Peninsula.

Nonetheless, one could not simply consign to the pages of history a line which had such a distinctive character and was held in so much affection by so many people.

In this final chapter the author will consider the line as it is today, well over 50 years after its closure. The purpose of this chapter is to examine ways in which the line, and memories of the line have been kept alive, demonstrating how, to the people of the Manhood, the tramway is not just a bygone relic but continues to stamp its influence on the local community. Firstly, literature on the tramway will be considered as this is an obvious point of reference for most people; then the *Selsey Tram Inn*; and finally the Jubilee Walk along the line.

1 Kenward and other Writers

Being part of the British railway network during some very important decades of railway history, it is inevitable that the tramway should be mentioned, if only some-times in passing, in a number of railway books. Apart from this book, only two have been written specifically about the line: Vic Mitchell and Keith Smith's *Branch Line to Selsey* in their popular Middleton Press series, and Edward Griffith's privately published booklet, *The Selsey Tramways*, which has been out of print for some time. Of equal importance, however, in obtaining an idea of the line's atmosphere and characters is a novel by James Kenward entitled *The Manewood Line*. It was written very soon after the line closed down, but sadly is now out of print and copies are scarce. Only one library copy is available throughout West Sussex. The author's intention was not to provide a gripping read, rather to introduce the reader to one of the great number of little railways which had overnight become 'derelict and turned into country lanes with grass growing over them, willow and elder beginning to prise sleepers apart, ballast hidden under heat-loving little flowers, and the all-conquering petrol engine turning the routes into roads of garages, bungalows and mock-Tudor tearooms'. The line chosen was, of course, the Selsey Tramway. The author made no attempt to conceal this, with Sidlesham for his purposes becoming 'Sillesham', Hunston 'Hunestan', and with Ferry and Mill Pond remaining the same. Selsey became 'Manewood', Chichester 'Munger' – a palindrome of the Roman name 'Regnum'.

The story is divided into two distinct parts, following a historical introduction: we are introduced in the first part to a group of characters who have connections with, and whose lives are touched by the line; in the second we meet a couple who visit the area on holiday, and are so captivated by the little line that they buy it and resurrect it. Soon the line runs with just the same unpredictability and bizarreness that characterised it before its closure.

There is clear historic authority for many of the incidents in the book. The line is described as having a 'serpentine course, bringing unheard of prosperity to the villages'. The 1910 floods are described graphically: 'the tide came up, hissing through the old harbour mouth, floating away stakes, overflowing the estuary, finding out ancient pools, pulling the railway lines askew and submerging them'. So is the 1923 accident: 'the engine lurched away off her course: there was a scream of out-thrust metals – the whole train shuddered as the wheel flanges bit into the sleepers and the engine bucked off the track'. And the sad scene that existed following the line's closure: 'In the farthest gloom amid the rusty drills, the cones of iron filings and mounds of cotton waste stood the *Munger*, rusty, blistered, her throttle control bound fast by spider's webs, a martin's nest secure under the cab roof'. Kenward alludes to 'decayed, oil-sodden sleepers', the cathedral spire seen from afar, 'quivering like a stalk of grass'; and writing of users of the line in the latter years, 'only summer visitors, occasionally for a joke, walked to some little halt at a lane-end to be driven through the fields'.

Other tales are more apocryphal, like that of the schoolboy who 'if he missed the passenger train after school would go home on the "coal and milk", dodging the swedes and cabbages the farmworkers would lob up for the driver and guards as the train went by'; the guard who changed his button hole using flowers which grew beside the track; the woman who having been told that a train was delayed owing to the driver having 'lost a pin off the engine' produced half a dozen safety pins to enable the journey to continue; and the woman who sympathised with the driver whose 'terrible bad hand' had delayed the train, only to find later that the 'terrible bad hand' was about to lose him the last three tricks in a game of bridge which was being played by the train personnel. Allusion is also made to a postcard showing an 'old engine with a mile-long smoke stack, kettle for a steamdome and a squirrel on a lead clopping along after'. It would be interesting to know if such a postcard ever existed.

The experiences of William and Mary, the couple who are the heroes of the second half of the story, and their comments thereon, cannot be far removed from the experiences and comments of any observer of the line. Mary's remark, 'You might lean out and pick thistledown clock to tell you the time', seems strangely similar to the joke (see Appendix One) about the flower growing in the time it takes to get to Selsey and back. William, speculating why it would take certain trains two minutes to do a stretch of line, according to the timetable, and others take one, wonders: 'Does the engine get tired there? Does the driver's mother have to get out halfway? Or does he stop to pick a bunch of flowers for his wife?'. The vista from Hunestan station following closure is particularly graphic: 'The Line curved out into a wilderness towards the tangled heart of the Manewood: the old timetable, its edges hanging down, revealing still older timetables beneath: the sleepers often invisible, under sorrell, vetch, hopclover, speedwell, white campion as ceal and flat as new notepaper'.

William goes to the derelict coaches and leans out, thinking of the days when those coaches went 'by the Manewood Country', with its 'ricks, lanes, bonds shaken by starlight under the hedges, the halts and the little inns'. He is so moved by this

92. The sorry remains of the canal drawbridge. Note the cathedral in the background, a welcome sight for Chichester-bound travellers.

93. The remains of the rife bridge, just north of Ferry.

94. The charming view from what used to be the trackbed, beside Pagham harbour.

that he decides to buy the railway and reopen it, but in what could only be described as Gilbertian terms. He enthuses:

> That's the point of the idea, don't you see? the inconvenience, that's going to be the attraction. We'll have cows specially trained to wander up and down the line, and a guard specially trained to get left behind, and a man with a little flag to go ahead at the level crossings. People'll love that: they'll love antiques and inconvenience, and we'll give them both. But of course we'll charge extra for it. The overheads'll be ridiculously low because any breakdown'll be quite in the picture. There'll be an advertisement – 'Passengers are invited to get out and pick blackberries on the line'. We won't cut down any of the bushes or flowers. Besides – it'll save expense. They shall be jolted and rattled, they shall bang their heads and miss their appointments.

He obtained two engines for the revived line, the *Camel* and the *Dromedary*, built, like the *Selsey*, specially for the line (and doubtless not foreseeing any further engines being built for it!): and some trucks 'like family pews, ludicrous and lovely'. An opening ceremony was planned with guests being invited to don Victorian period costume. Inns close to the line were to be given apposite names: *The Rocket, The 2-4-0, The Guard's Van Let Loose, The Two Hours Overdue, The Broken Coupling* and *The Merry Driver*. Advertisements appeared: the 'longest, most expensive and slowest route to Munger'; 'Thistledown Clocks – Passengers may alight here to discover the time'.

'At every level crossing', we are told, 'crowds blocked the road, and during the waiting excited Manewood men would buttonhole the stranger and tell him tales of guards racing against the driver, of the driver's 'terrible bad hand', of a safety pin used to repair the engine, of a squirrel and numerous others'.

Kenward's book ends happily. William is able to laugh in the face of the writer of a railway's typical obituary: 'A little railway of peculiar fascination is to finish its working life ... all those who have visited the town will learn with regret ... surely the strangest little railway in all England'.

The reality, of course, is very different. There has been no resurrection, no resurgence, no entrepreneurs with the courage, and dare one say it, the fool-hardiness to proceed with a scheme of this sort. Yet the point Kenward makes still holds good. To have reopened the line and to have attempted to instil in it the regimentation and uniformity of one of the main lines would have been to rob of it of the character and individuality and consequently the affection with which it was held. Kenward did students of the line a great service. He has provided a valuable reference point and brought history to life, and even if the writing is not scholarly it is readable, and does indeed transport the student of the line back in time both humorously and sympathetically.

2 *The Selsey Tram Inn*
No other single landmark in the area is more tangible or obvious proof of the existence of the Selsey Tram than this hostelry, which is situated on the busy A286 Chichester to Wittering road in Donnington, barely a mile from the centre of the city and on a road which is used by all those travelling to the popular bathing and surfing centres of Bracklesham and the Witterings. One might expect the inn to have been

95. The railway's present connection with Selsey, an old Pullman carriage, now a house. The tramway was an obvious means of transporting the carriage down to Selsey, although it is clear that low-loaders were used to transport some by road.

built during the time that the line was still functioning, possibly standing by one of the principal stations, like any other railway hotel. It is thus surprising to learn that the inn was not opened to the public until 1968; it does not actually border on the track at all; and the decision was not taken to name it the *Selsey Tram* until quite a number of legal formalities connected with its opening had been carried out.

When the inn opened in February 1968 it was managed by Brickwoods; by 1987, however, the house was part of Roast Inns Division of Whitbread. The plans show that the two bars were given names with railway overtones – the Pullman Bar and the Station Bar – with the restaurant area being called the Dining Car. There is no evidence that these names have survived, and certainly no visitor would be aware of them.

Incidentally, it is interesting to note that a modern estate in Hunston, built very close to the line, has been named Tramway Close. A group of houses in Church Road, Selsey, were known as Tramway Cottages but they have since been numbered and the name has fallen into disuse.

3 The Jubilee Walk

Whilst certain stretches of the line are still reasonably easy to discern, there are large stretches which are far harder to trace, and harder still, if not impossible, to walk over. Any opportunity, therefore, to walk the privately owned and cultivated stretches with the blessing of the landowners is not to be scoffed at, and on Sunday 1 May 1977, just such an opportunity arose.

The promoters of this historic event were not railway buffs nor were they railway ramblers, whose work in reopening stretches of disused railway to pedestrians has only recently expanded into a major leisure interest. They were in fact the Good Companions, a Sidlesham-based charity who suggested the walk as a means of raising money to buy a new minibus for transporting the housebound in the area. The date selected was not especially significant, but the year perhaps was, being the 80th anniversary of the line's opening, and the Silver Jubilee year of the reign of Her Majesty Queen Elizabeth the Second.

Not only was it hoped that the Good Companions would raise a goodly sum. As the secretary, Brigadier André, put it, it gave an opportunity for walkers to explore the 'exceptionally beautiful countryside which the normal traveller of the Manhood area is not able to appreciate' by covering the old route there and back on foot – a total of 15 miles.

Appropriately enough, the then mayor, Patrick Combes, started the walk, and in doing so bemoaned the lack of a footplate which would have enabled him to emulate Alderman Ballard back in 1897! The Good Companions entered fully into the spirit of the occasion, dressing up as Victorian railway staff, Brigadier André being the station master at Hunston for the day. The Selsey Lions and Sidlesham Football Club helped out with administration and refreshments, while the Football Club erected bunting. About thirty marshals were used altogether, disguised as station masters, wheeltappers and platelayers. Their duties on this day had nothing to do with trains, of course: their brief was to see that walkers kept to the track without spoiling the crops, positioning red flags to ensure the roads were crossed safely (shades of the early '30s) and keeping walkers from stray golf balls whilst walking past the links. They were also on hand to point out items of interest. Stanley Richards, who had a long association with the line when it was actually functioning, remarked: 'Never in my wildest dreams did I expect to be promoted to station master at Sidlesham!' The

96. A railway rambler's paradise. The straight, clearly defined tramway route between Golf Links Halt and Ferry, in unspoilt, scenic surroundings.

cottage near the station at Chalder became a refreshment room and exhibition hall. A minibus and ambulance service was provided.

As the *Chichester Observer* reported, 'They strode, they ran, they even marched. The old came with sticks and the young in push chairs [covering] up to 14 hot miles' walking so that others might ride in comfort'. A total of over 400 took part, including a contingent of Military Police. The oldest entrant was a 92-year-old man named Charles Gunn who had taken part in the Antwerp Olympics of 1920! Special mention was made of a 72-year-old man named Mr. Bonner who raised £100 in sponsorship money.

It was not possible to retrace exactly the old route from start to finish, but the route remained as faithful as it could be, thanks largely to the co-operation of the local farmers and other landowners. However, it was noted at the time that they would be 'reluctant to allow such a walk again' and that this was a 'once in a lifetime chance'. It remains to be seen whether or not that prophecy is borne out. This particular walk achieved what it set out to do; the Good Companions were able to proceed with the ordering of the new bus.

Conclusion

Standing at the spot where Mill Pond Halt used to be, and looking towards Chalder, across acres of intensively farmed countryside, the idea that earlier in this century a train once ran, carrying not just a handful but often vast crowds of passengers, seems quite laughable. Disbelief is perhaps temporarily lifted when viewing the long strip of embankment between the sites of Sidlesham and Ferry, but when standing at the junction of Manor Road and Denshare Road, and at the sprawling areas of nearby housing which now occupy the old route, it is simply ridiculous to attempt to recall the days of packed coaches and railbuses drawing up at the Town station with Mr. Wingham waiting to convey passengers into the centre of Selsey or to the *Selsey Hotel.*

There are, as the years go on, fewer and fewer who remember the tramway in operation. In due course it will become impossible for anyone to say with confidence that they have travelled on that line. There will be nobody who can say that they stood patiently waiting at the little rural halts for a train which might turn up if the driver remembered to get up; that one day, when they were late for the train, they sent their nearest and dearest along to the station to ask the driver to wait: or that they were amongst class 3B at their Chichester school who kept missing first lesson during the early part of 1911. No passengers will be able to recall standing watching sadly at the window as the driver remonstrated with the driver of a car into whom their loco had just smashed; sitting patiently in their railcar whilst Mr. Pullinger's mousetraps were placed in the luggage van: or being thrown out of their seats one September morning in 1923. No witnesses will be able to testify to watching with quiet amusement the raging of the station master as a couple of railmen launched into the chorus of *The Sidlesham Snail*: sitting disconsolately quite unable to finish a piece of correspondence because of the jolting and jogging of their Shefflex: or looking anxiously at the *Morous* each time to see how much of its new coat of paint had worn away during last night's thunderstorm. Even now, few can say with confidence that they sat in their carriage as it made its ponderous way through the isolated communities of the Manhood, watching the bus speeding past it, deciding that in future that would be how they got to work.

Yet could it be that some day in the future, the whistle of locomotive units will again be heard on the Manhood? Will the flat landscape, only punctuated by the soaring spire of Chichester cathedral, and so often becalmed in a mysterious, perhaps eerie hush, make way for yet another intrusion of man?

The demand for good communication between Chichester and Selsey has never been greater. Though Selsey remains an unpretentious, unspectacular place, still a place which one cannot go beyond, only back whence one came, it is fully established as a large active community. On a normal, unremarkable Monday lunchtime in

October, the writer travelled from Chichester to Selsey, a journey of about fifteen minutes, and was passed by over 80 vehicles travelling in the opposite direction. This alone represents at least 80 potential passengers, possibly many more. A 1991 campaigner for a proper bridleway between Chichester and Selsey, which he suggested might incorporate some of the old line, estimated 12,000 vehicles used this road each day: it has been described as the busiest B road in the south. Buses are frequent and well used.

These factors alone offer two grounds for hope amongst those yearning for a return to rail travel on the Manhood. Firstly, the traffic is borne by just one road. With the increase in population, it is conceivable that a time will come when the B2145 will be unable to cope. Indeed during 1991 cyclists presented a petition to the Mayor of Chichester demanding a cycle route to enable them to travel from Selsey to Chichester in safety. The B2145 is narrow in places with at least two treacherous bends. The increase in traffic and the consequent likelihood of intolerable congestion or accident is likely to drive many other pressure groups to seek an alternative means of getting from one place to the other.

Secondly, there is increasing concern about pollution caused by motor vehicles. Concern for the environment has since the late 1980s become a major political and social issue at every level. Rail travel offers one obvious alternative to the motor cars with their uneconomical consumption of fuel and injection of substances into the atmosphere which not only pollute the surroundings but contribute to global warming.

A rail link between Chichester and Selsey would not only ease the traffic congestion; it would be less environmentally unfriendly too, and there is no doubt that it would be well-used. It would, of course, need to be fast, frequent and reliable to compete with the buses. Indeed, it would need to provide viable competition to the buses just in the same way that the buses gave competition to the tramway.

In order to be a success, the bad habits of its forebears would have to be subdued. There could be no oversleeping, no cows encroaching on the line, no stopping for late passengers or animal feed, no acquisition of 50-year-old rolling stock, no risks of accidents with motor vehicles, no temperamental drawbridges, and proper protection against the vagaries of the weather. These factors may seem endearing and fun to read about now, but in these times, just as in the 1920s and 1930s, to ignore the economic realities and so-called market forces in organising the transport of passengers and freight is naive in the extreme. Colonel Stephens and his team learnt that to their cost towards the end of the tramway's time; any entrepreneur today would very quickly learn the same hard lesson.

Yet it would be a shame to end this study of this remarkable line with stark prosaic pragmatism. It is precisely the quirks and oddities of Colonel Stephens' operation which make such a study so entertaining and rewarding, and few, if any, readers would wish to deny a secret longing to be transported through the still, open fields of the peninsula perhaps hauled by the *Morous* or *Hesperus*, cows carelessly chewing their cud and within inches of the path of the train, the sound of Emidio Guarnacchio enthusing over his ice-cream sales, the crates of fresh lobster sitting temptingly in the nearby luggage compartment, the steady application of brakes as the locomotive pulled up at a deserted platform with hardly a house in sight ...

97.   Something many spectators would remember – black smoke belching from the tramway. A train headed by *Ringing Rock* crossing tramway bank in 1934-5.

The Course of the Tramway Today

Those readers, who feel sufficiently moved by what they have already read to explore for traces of the line, will largely be disappointed. Only three pieces of evidence of the tramway's existence remain: the drawbridge abutments at Hunston, and station platforms at Hunston and Chalder. To this could notionally be added the scanty remains of the rife crossing just north of Ferry.

Only three stretches of the old route can be walked, namely the stretches between the A286 at Stockbridge and the point at which the tramway left the canal; the draw-bridge remains north of Hunston and the B2145 at Hunston; and from Mill Lane, on the edge of Pagham Harbour, along the harbour edge to the B2145 at Ferry Corner. The rest of the route is neither accessible to the public nor discernible other than for tiny fragments.

For the most part, intensive farming and other development has obliterated traces of the tramway. Beginning at Chichester, the route of the line follows wasteland behind the gardens of houses in Terminus Road. Passing through part of the Terminus Road Industrial Estate, it hugs the fields of the Girls' High School, then, crossing the bypass, continues through the residential area of Stockbridge, crossing the A286 and striking south-eastwards through new housing development to reach the Chichester Canal. Running parallel to the canal for a while, it strikes out across fields, over the canal and past the rear end of the large modern housing estates which comprise Hunston. Having crossed the B2145 Chichester - Selsey road, the route runs parallel with it across farmland, before curving south-eastwards across the golf course past the redbrick buildings of Hoe Farm, and then swinging south-westwards across more farmland, passing Chalder and skirting the village of

Sidlesham. The route, totally unrecognisable in the flat fields, crosses Rookery Lane at the site of Mill Pond Halt, and here forsakes farmland for the marshlands (owned by Souhern Water) at the northern end of Pagham Harbour, skirting the housing estate at Manhood Lane. At Mill Lane, which is crossed, the Pagham Nature Reserve is reached, and the route – here a public footpath – follows round the harbour to reach a rife which is crossed. The footpath ceases and the route continues up to the B2145 again, passing the site of Ferry Station. It then crosses a short stretch of farmland before striking through the gorse on the fringes of Selsey Golf Links. Having crossed Golf Links Lane, the route goes across a field and under the B2145, ending its journey in the cluster of modern housing development at the back of Elm Tree Close. The route of the extension to Selsey Beach is situated between Mount-wood Road and Beach Road ending by Manor Lane. The terrain throughout is flat.

It is perfectly possible to follow existing rights of way and remain within sight of the old route throughout with a few very limited exceptions, and both the old route and a continuous chain of appropriate rights of way suitable for walkers (though not horse-riders) are shown on the maps, as are points of particular interest to tramway explorers. A separate publication describing such a walk in a format suitable for walkers is in preparation.

This section, dealing as it does with the transition from railway to wasteland to other uses, would be incomplete without the poem written by Winifred Langer of the East Manhood Women's Institute in 1990, concerning the revival of the Pagham Harbour Nature Reserve.

From Pollution to Paradise

A rat-infested hole where flies abound;
The trainless track beside the swampy ground,
Where trucks of rubbish, brought from miles around
Drop metal, paper, bottles on a mound.

The seagulls gathered from the tidal bay;
The smells kept butterflies and bees away;
Then men brought soil and smothered all from day,
And grass and flowers wild began to stay.

Migrating birds came down to rest and feast:
So after twenty years the train had ceased;
The empty track was walked those years at least,
A free footpath was made for friends and beast.

At ease beside the marsh, where twice a day,
The sea pours in, where traffic is away,
So man and nature dream around the bay,
The Sidlesham Reserve has come to stay.

Environmentalists might care to note that not a single yard of the tramway has become a dumping ground for 'trucks of rubbish ... from miles around'. However, the variety of present day usage – playing fields, housing, farming, golf courses and back gardens – makes it all the harder for the tramway explorer to discover traces of the old line.

Appendix One

Reminiscences

It is not surprising that the Selsey Tramway by its very nature has caused a lot of its customers, as well as writers of that time, to commit to paper their thoughts and reflections on the line.

A 'letter from Selsey' talks of: 'the funny little railway' and goes on, 'nowhere in all my travels have I met its counterpart save in Brittany where Sooty Lizzie took its smoky way through fields from Dinard to the golf course of San Briac [*sic*]'.

Harriet James, writing to the *West Sussex Gazette* in February 1935 shortly after closure, described the line as 'novel and exciting' for schoolchildren, although she imagined exacting grown-ups held other views. She wrote of the line's playful eccentricities 'feeling sorry for those in the prosaic, reliable omnibus'. Like Mrs. James, many others recalling the line in modern times have to go back to their childhood for memories of witnessing it. One such person is Vernon Fogden who recalls:

> The train was part of my life. When I was quite young, the house at Donnington Bridge was empty and we used to play in it. Several of us used to get down between the sleepers on the bridge and watch the motor trains go over our heads. If we got a speck of oil drop on us it was as good as a V.C. My sisters used to go to school from Chalder at Miss Portsmouth's schools in one of the Pallants. My father said that [the opening of a] milk transporting business at Flagstones, Hunston, was the last straw for the tram. We used to use Hunston station as headquarters for 'Nicky Nicky show your light'. A very expensive hobby as you had to own a torch.

A Mrs. Proudly, following the walk in 1977, wrote:

> I would like to say how much I enjoyed the walk to Selsey on 1 May. It brought back memories of the times I went on the old tram. We always had one day's outing in the summer from St John's Church on the Tram to Selsey. It was the only day out for us, so it meant a lot to us. We always made a joke of it as it went so slow. We said you could put your plants in going down and pick the flowers on the way back. Still, we enjoyed it.

A Mrs. Terry recalled in September 1976 how she paid 'two or three coppers' to travel on the line. She stated she disliked travelling by the canal because the tramway seemed too close to the canal bank! She recalls a hunchbacked station master named Michael Baker.

In response to a broadcast by 'Chichester Area Talking News for the Blind and Partially Sighted', the following letter was received from Mrs. Henrietta Conduit of Selsey:

113

Having enjoyed the article on the Selsey tram, I feel I must write a few reminiscences of my own. For many years my family visited Selsey every Easter, returning in October, and so I can remember the excitement of my sister and I as children, arriving at Chichester main station, and from there the fun began. We were trundled across what is now the car park which then was the shunting lines and sheds; with dog, cabin trunks and numerous boxes, arriving at a little corrugated iron hut waiting room for the Selsey Tram to arrive. When the little Tram puffed in with an engine and about three carriages, we would all pile in and set off on our blissful journey. The guard, splendidly attired in full uniform adorned with gold braid, with a fresh carnation buttonhole every day, welcomed each of us to Selsey telling us of all the points of interest. He was a great Sussex character! When the two little buses took over, running back to back, they put a little flat truck in between them to carry the luggage; and sometimes we kids were allowed to ride on the truck sitting on the trunks. I still remember the thrill of riding over the banks of Sidlesham harbour. I did rush to see the accident, which was very sad, when it went off the rails. It was very upsetting for everybody when the fireman was killed.

A Mr. A. Earwicker writes of the excitement of using the tram to go on a shopping spree, the tram passing Hoe Farm, where butter would be put aboard, and 'Mr. Hudson's windmill'. He continues:

my father would often be shaving in readiness to go to Chichester. When we heard the Tram whistle blow at Ferry he knew if he ran down Mill Lane he would miss the train, so he dashed across the meadow. The engine driver would see him running and would stop the Tram for my father to jump aboard.

Incidentally Mrs. Langer, who recalls a Sunday school outing from Portsmouth to the tramway, also tells of boys being sent on ahead to 'knock up' intending passengers, the train waiting for them if they were not quite ready.

A Mr. Barker says, 'I remember going to Hoe Farm for school holidays: when "Bumpity Bump" was stopped by request to drop me at the little platform at Hoe Farm, the driver blew a whistle blast to announce our arrival'. He recalls Farmer Jupp at Hoe Farm, who weighed 28 stone.

Another correspondent referred to the tram guard as a

human, pleasant person, ready to let us have our amusements as long as the carriage was not otherwise occupied and no other passengers were annoyed. We held concerts, frequently singing in chorus all the songs we knew – sometimes even forgot to hush when we stopped at a station. Some of the most exciting, loveliest games of Blind Man's Buff ever played were carried on by us in these carriages, with their low wooden seats, while the tram was in motion.

Former employees of the tramway have their memories too. Alfred Robinson recalls how sometimes as a worker on the railway he overslept and the train had to wait as a consequence. He says that working on the railway had some compensations, including fine home brewed beer which the mother of one of his colleagues made, which they shared between them with their dinner. He tells of how, when he asked for an increase in his pay, which was just 16s. 8d. per week, he was told the company could not afford to pay him any more. He would use the line to travel to Sidlesham to meet his girlfriend, whom he eventually married. She was doubtless impressed by the ice-cream he used to take on the train for her.

Stanley Richards recalls how, when serving in the Middle East during the First World War, he received sacks of hay for the horses which had been stamped 'Chalder Farm'. Ironically he first started working on the tramway as clerk and ticket collector. On Sundays, when there was no passenger service, he worked as a stoker on engines pulling trucks of hay and corn, acquired by the War Office from Manhood Farmers.

Tim Johnson recalls that he held the speed record, having got from Chichester to Selsey on the Sidlesham engine in 18 minutes.

Other line users confine their observations to the line's primitive working methods and equipment which were, of course, easy sources of witty and descriptive writing. An early user of the line described Hunston station thus:

> Imagine, O reader, an elevated platform supported by four rough timber piles and a small cistern with a pump thereon, the latter being assiduously worked by a small boy in his shirtsleeves, whistling and happy. A pipe led down into a little stream trickling in a ditch by the side of the road, from which the small boy pumped up water with all his might. It was a scene of pastoral and sweet simplicity.

The writer went on to say that this whole performance caused the road to be blocked for nine minutes, and caused a dog cart to wait. There was a 'scornful expression' on the face of the horse, and the driver gave a look 'that could only be translated by a word far too impolite to insert in these pages'. The cows adjoining the line, says the writer, 'expressed painful contempt of the modern railway enterprise'. Despite having done the two miles from Chalder to Sidlesham in 'grand style', the writer's train, perhaps partially due to a complex shunting operation at Sidlesham, reached Selsey 45 minutes late. 'I am told', he says, 'that the Company did not state the arrival times of trains. I am rather surprised that they do so now – It is an over-bold stroke of policy'. Interestingly, the writer talks of the line traversing a portion of country 'where the tide used to sweep'. In 1910, of course, the tide was to sweep again. Another witness to the pumping boy at Hunston remembers an occasion on which the perched lad's services were not required, leaving the boy in question with a 'sad and disconsolate look on his face, unwanted and ignored'.

A Dr. Nichol, writing in September 1932, recalls a journey in a steam train headed by *Morous* with an ex-Southern Region coach and some goods trucks. He was the only passenger. He recalls an extra 12 minutes being allowed to attach or detach wagons at appropriate points. The train left Chichester five minutes late and pulled up for 'some belated person'; he suggested this might be a railway official. One 'attaching' exercise involved the incorporation of an empty wagon between the locomotives and the front coach. Selsey Town station presented, says Nicol, 'a cheerful appearance after a sight of the rotting, deserted platforms elsewhere'.

Of the Shefflexes, a Mr. Edmond Venables recalls: 'The driver sat on a sort of hole at floor level with his legs dangling over the track – the conductor climbed from truck to truck to take the fares'.

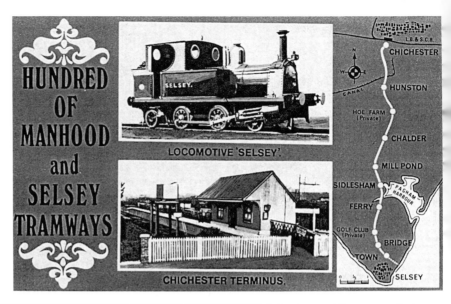

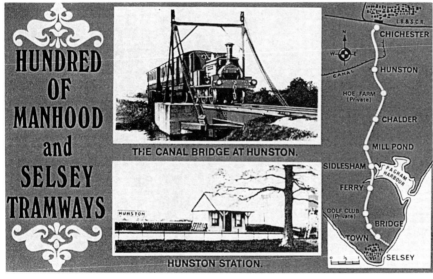

98a, b & c. Three attractively presented reminders of the tramway for the latter day connoisseur.

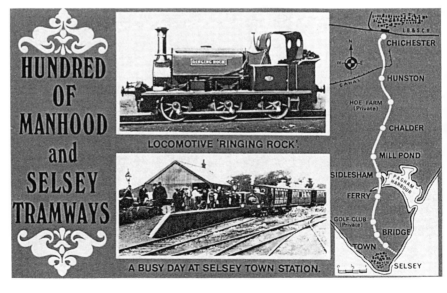

The line's idiosyncrasies were not always well received. Cyril Carver recalls how, when it was wet, the train would have difficulty in climbing up to Kipson Bank, just south of Hunston. Passengers would have to get out and walk up the track to the top.

A Mr. Haynes recalls how 'morning by morning' the engine refused to budge – 'much time was taken getting it to start'.

There was one person however who did benefit from the line's rural and easy-going nature. Mr. Hawkins, the owner of an allotment near the line recalls how he fed onions on the manure from the cattle trucks. The onions were enormous!

Charles Fidler tells how he would go to Chichester on the train as a goalkeeper with Selsey Football Club. The train would run out of steam and this inevitably caused delay before the journey could go on.

So much for individual users. The press also had a great deal to say about this unusual line. The *Hampshire Telegraph* wrote: 'To start a journey from either end was by no means to feel sure that you would reach your destination; and little mishaps sometimes happened which made the timetable far less reliable than anything which could be complained of in connection with the new service on the Southern Railway'. This was written just after the grant of the Light Railway Order – the *Telegraph* saw considerable possibilities for railway development in the Manhood area. 'A step forward', they said, 'in the direction of improving the grass-grown track and giving it something approaching the status of railway would undoubtedly be an aid to the development and improvement which is otherwise going on in every direction'.

The *Daily Chronicle* wrote that although there was nothing very remarkable about the mainline journey to Chichester,

> if you're not very careful, you'll miss [the Tramway station at Chichester] because it consists of a wooden hut. The train for Selsey is a cross between two railway carriages of the days of Stephenson, and two very obsolete Tram cars of the early '80s. The guard seems to be a kind of Pooh Bah official – a combination of guard, stationmaster, ticket distributor and superintendent. With great creaking and groaning and rattling of chains, the train crawls out of Chichester to the shrieking of a strident whistle. You stop at stations where there are not any houses, and houses where there are not any stations, and if you are in luck you reach Selsey the same day that you start, To reach Selsey Bill you must travel into the land of severe simplicity.

A more caustic assessment appears in a series of newspaper articles called 'Selsey Billets':

> Visitors making their first trip to Selsey by the Trans-Peninsular Tramway must receive many amusing impressions of the stations en route and imagine for the moment that they were being carried into the back of beyond. After being bumped over a track red with rust, they eventually cross a bleak and desolate stretch of moorland and arrive at the Ferry where a dilapidated structure like a cross between a cowshed and a kennel is perched jauntily on an antiquated platform and does duty as a waiting room. If it wasn't for the honour of the thing I would prefer to wait in the rain.

The *Chichester Observer*, in February 1909, described it as the 'noisiest and most rickety railway in England', stating that the line 'runs, no crawls, between Chichester and Selsey'; in March 1965 described it as 'surely the oddest of railways and which probably suffered more breakdown and mishap than any other Line in the country' and stated that 'conversation is almost impossible'.

The *West Sussex Gazette* of January 1935 called it, in its prime, 'the only serviceable means of regular communication between the villages of the Selsey peninsula and the rest of the world, the single track wandering across roads and fields to curious and isolated little stations'.

In 1907 the *Hampshire Telegraph* expressed the hope that the light railway would be 'merged in the Brighton system' and that 'important trains will travel over the Line bearing happy freights of parents and children to the ideal seaside place of Selsey on sea'. It referred to the 'toy trains' of the Hundred of Manhood and Selsey Tramway 'rattling along' past farms and golf links.

The *Chichester Observer* in March 1965 stated that it would 'probably now be a money spinner, particularly in summer.'

What a contrast, therefore, with the bland, cheerless, electrical multiple units plying the Sussex railways today. Punctuality and passenger comfort may have improved radically – although for some even that assertion might be the subject of fierce debate! – but what the reminiscences show is not merely a recognition of the slowness and discomfort of the journey, but also a deep affection for its peculiarities and eccentricities. In short, the relationship between the line and its users could be said to have been like the relationship between a disobedient child and its mother: a great love for the child combined with resigned tolerance of his or her disobedient behaviour. To the writers quoted above, closure of the line must have brought with it feelings similar to those experienced by a parent whose child has been snatched from its loving grasp.

Appendix Two

Eyewitness Account

As the Selsey Tram becomes more and more distant in the memory, so are there fewer and fewer people who remember it. At the time of writing, an adult user of the line would now be in his mid-seventies. Nevertheless, there are people who do remember it well, and who hold it in very great affection, for all its faults. One such person is Mr. Green, who lives in Selsey. The author went to visit him at his home one chilly afternoon in early February. Mr. Green started with a very personal memory:

G: We used to lay underneath the platform and put pins – you know, the straight pins on the line, so that they would get crushed flat.

DB: Did any of you ever get hurt?

G: Oh no, no. We kept our heads well out of the way. When the train moved to Chichester or to here it flattened all the needles or pins – you know, the old fashioned pins.

DB: Did you travel on the line?

G: Oh, yes. Eight pence return, Sidlesham to Chichester. We used to go and get the weekend meat from Shippams in South Street. Mr. Porter there used to be the local vet and used to come out to Sidlesham if anybody's animals were not well – on a Sunday morning, probably, most times.

DB: The trains themselves: what were they like?

G: Three carriages and the engine.

DB: I've seen some amazing pictures of Shefflexes.

G: That's it. They came after the accident: the man got killed. On the Sunday night previous we were, my mother and sister and us three boys, came down to the Selsey gas works. My stepbrother came on duty of a Friday night – wouldn't come home till Monday morning, and we used to come down on the train and walk through the meadows to his gas works, and [laugh] on the Sunday night we had to walk back to Sidlesham on the railway line, but there was a footpath at the side so we were quite clear, and my mother, she said to us, 'one of these days', she said, 'that tram is coming off the line' and it happened the very next morning. The first tram out of Selsey, that was, at 8 o'clock. But it could have been saved if the guard had been in his place, you know, near the winding wheel. That was what upset the railway altogether.

DB: It became bankrupt in 1931, didn't it?

G: Yes, and in the meantime they were using motor – the old Fords. They had two of them, back to back, with a little truck between them, and then when the Shefflexes were bought they, I assume they did, came up from Tonbridge in Kent. That was where Colonel Stephens lived.

DB: Were the carriages comfortable to ride in?

G: Oh yes, beautiful and comfortable. Really better than today's buses are.

DB: Was it quite a smooth ride?

G: Oh yes. You wouldn't know you were going along, bar the clickety click. And on Sundays before my stepfather went to work on the golf course, he was one of the fire-men, they used to bring out an engine with about twelve trucks on it which would stop outside Sidlesham station, and father would look after the fire, and the driver, he was the local preacher by the name of Charlie Mould, he used to come with a white glove on so that when he was turning the bible pages he wouldn't mark them.

DB: The trains themselves: were they fairly reliable?

G: Oh yes. When it first started it was very up to date. Then they put in a loop line at Sidlesham because when the motor tram was used that used to go on the sidings, and the main tram when it came from Chichester down, it would go on the straight, normal run.

DB: They used to run on time?

G: Oh yes. The first went out of Selsey at eight in the morning and by the time they got back it was nine o'clock.

DB: An hour for the round trip?

G: Yes, by the time they'd taken in water and picked up all the goods at Chichester main station. My meat used to come on the train from Portsmouth at 7 o'clock. I'd get it outside of Sidlesham station by 9 o'clock. Hindquarter beef, a sack with two tins of liver in it, one of lamb's and one of pig's and so many sheep, you know, lambs – frozen.

DB: So it wasn't just passengers?

G: Oh no, coal, they used to carry down coal to Selsey, you see, and en route they dropped so many trucks at Hunston, so many trucks at Chalder, so many trucks at Sidlesham, and bring all the rest down to Selsey.

DB: So when the line stopped they had to find other means to do that?

G: Oh yes. That's when the coal went up. I mean, we were only paying about two shillings to half a crown a bag.

DB: And when the line closed, it all went on to the roads?

G: Yes, that's when it started to go up, you know, in price.

DB: Do you think it was because of the Chichester to Selsey road that the line started to decline? People had more cars ...

G: Oh yes, I mean when the motor trams started running on the rails, the conductor had to get out and get a red flag and stand in the road to show the flag.

DB: Do you recall the closing ceremony?

G: Yes, I was home. It was on a Saturday afternoon when the last engine was towed up and they transferred it to the main line.

DB: It must have been very sad.

G: Oh terrible. Of course they hooted. Ray Apps, one of the firemen then, he got his driver to keep hooting. It was a sad day because we used to enjoy it. During the summer months they used to pick up children from Littlehampton in big coaches, longer coaches – what do you call – Pullman coaches. They were beautiful. They brought the children down, with one engine on the front and one pushing behind. They'd bring about four coaches.

DB: It meant the line was well used.

G: Oh yes. At Sidlesham the ganger, the head man who looked after the line, lived in a railway coach. He had his meals and all in it. He slept there, and everything else.

DB: Isn't it right that in Sidlesham, where you lived, the line used to go quite close?

G: Oh yes. You only had to get over the wall and walk across a field like a meadow – and there we were, right on the track.

DB: Was there a station master at Sidlesham?

G: Oh no, it was unstaffed. But they had a one-line telephone all the way from Selsey to Chichester, you see, and you could hear the bell ring. So when the door was left open, we used to go in and listen to the conversation. Then there was a man by the name of Mr. Barnes, he took over as ganger, and he lived next door to us. We could hear all the messages. They extended the line by putting up two posts. His wife used to receive the calls. There might be damage or fires; you could have a fire on the side of the line. Yes, it was a sad day when the whole of the railway closed.

DB: So by that time you were still going up to Shippams on Saturday mornings?

G: Oh yes. We had to go by bus. We started going by bus, open decker, open top. If it rained you'd get wet!

DB: The buses were more expensive, weren't they?

G: They were 1s. 6d. return – Sidlesham to Chichester.

DB: So it was more expensive than going by train?

G: Oh yes.

DB: Were the trains fairly well used?

G: Oh yes. People used to go shopping, you see. Unless they came down to Selsey, they had to go to Chichester to get all the main supplies for their homes, and of course markets and everything else.

DB: It's not now a case of people coming in on the train and having to walk to the shops, so they need to be in the centre, as people can now go to these out of town places and load up their cars. It must have been nicer, mustn't it, just to get on the train and to ...

G: Yes, it was a day out for us lads, because we went up on the first tram which was about eight o'clock or about ten past eight. It'd arrive at Sidlesham station, and then we'd get aboard and we'd go up there and we'd come back on the 12 o'clock, so by the time we got back it was about half past twelve. It was a day's outing for us lads!

DB: Lovely. It must have been smashing. You had the whole morning in Chichester to look around the shops ...

G: That's right, and, you don't remember that, but in South Street there was a cinema called the Picturedrome, where 'Iceland' is now. And across the road was Fielder's garage and on Wednesdays, when they started the motor trains, a Mr. Baker, who lived down here, drove one of the trains – motors, it was the time they had the Shefflexes – it cost us 1s. 6d. and that included a free seat in the picturedrome.

DB: Inclusive?

G: Yes – and so we had – we used to collect the money, say three shillings, and we'd enough for fish and chip supper – so we'd come down on the rail, back at night, about ten o'clock or after, and eat fish and chips in the carriage.

DB: That probably explains something. When I was looking through the old timetables, I came across a train that left Chichester about ten o'clock on Wednesday nights, even though they usually stopped in the early evening.

G: That's right. That was what we used to call the Picture Train. We had girlfriends you know, and other boys, and Mr. Baker the driver would put the lights on the back carriage – you know, the back carriage of the two carriage trains – and [laugh] of course we used to do the snuggling ... oh yes, good old times, they were.

DB: So you were reliant on public transport – the trains and the buses when they started operating?

99. Might Mr. Green have been one this youthful crowd the tramway had just deposited at Selsey?

G: Oh yes. Harold Day – he lived over here – and a man named Edwards, he used to drive the double decker, and they never used to speak to each other.

DB: There must have been terrible rivalry.

G: Oh yes.

DB: You presumably used the line a lot when you were a youngster.

G: Oh yes. And after we left school we used the line because when we wanted to go out on these picture trips you only had to get in touch with the driver of any of the trams that passed through Sidlesham, and say 'So and so, six for tonight.' You'd leave all the arrangements to them. He knew about motors. He was an 'all in all', you know.

DB: What else can you tell me about the line and the trains?

G: When the engines used to stop at Sidlesham there was a big curve in the line. The engine used to put up force to get round the bend. They used to blow smoke out and hot ash, and used to set fire to the meadows round there.

DB: So pollution is nothing new?

G: Oh no. It was black! Oh the hay, they used to cut each side of the track from Selsey up to Chichester, then at weekends they used to pick it all up and let it dry and take it to Chichester main station. If you wanted a load of coke, it had to be brought out of Selsey by cart. They had a station at Ferry – it was only a shepherd's hut. When they came down to Chichester with the railway they had to be careful when they got nearly to the Ferry because there was a bridge over the actual rife, and it was on a bit of a bend, so they had to slacken down to get down there.

DB: Wasn't there another station – the Golf Club Halt?

G: Oh yes. That was put on for, like, McGlashan and people like that – big blokes as we used to call them. They used to come down to the golf links – it was an 18-hole course then. There was one platform, Golf Links Halt. At one time they had one at the Mill Pond at Sidlesham.

DB: Was it possible for a train to come off the main line and get on to the tram?

G: No, not the big railway engines. They didn't venture on. I'll tell you, and this is a true story too. A man, the guard, this lady said to the guard down here at Selsey, he said 'Do you think, Mr. Walker', she said, 'I will get to Chichester in time to catch the first train out to London?': 'Oh yes', he said. And the driver heard all the conversation at the engine, so he said to the fireman, 'slacken up! we won't go too fast'. So when they got to Chichester the mainline train had gone. So she goes up to Walker and said 'Mr. Walker, my train has gone!' The driver knew Walker had been tipped by her, hoping that he would tell the driver to keep moving. So she went to the driver and said 'Jocelyn, I've lost the train, and I tipped the guard'. 'Ah', he said, 'You've oiled the wrong end!'. I've always remembered that!

DB: Passengers always had to change trains?

G: Yes. They had to get out at Chichester and walk across to the main line.

DB: It wasn't proper advertised connections – you just had to take your chance?

G: Well, that's it. But Southern Railway, as it was then, they always had particulars of what time the trains came down from Chichester station to Selsey. All the staff that worked for the railway lived in cottages quite nearby. The station was where the *Selsey Hotel* is ... the *Stargazer*.

DB: After Patrick Moore!

G: Yes, oh him! [laughter]. But oh, we had some wonderful times on the track. Oh, when we were lads, you know, mother would say to us, 'Oh, they've brought some coal up in the trucks at Sidlesham. When they've emptied them, go before they pick the empties up to take them back to Chichester. See how much coal they've dropped'. You'd be surprised how many bucketfuls you'd get. Even though it was cheap, it was very useful.

DB: It sounds such a friendly line.

G: Oh yes, you knew everybody. Even the platelayers, the men who kept the line you know, all the maintenance of the line and that.

DB: So although the stations weren't staffed, there were plenty of people working on the line?

G: Oh, by the way: Sidlesham station is now moved, bit by bit, and taken to, you know the Runcton Walnut Tree? The other side of the road you'll find a bungalow – that's Sidlesham station. [Mr. Green is almost certainly mistaken; there is no bungalow in Runcton resembling Sidlesham station]. It was moved timber by timber, of course. It was galvanised tin, the actual station.

DB: As far as Colonel Stephens, was concerned: was he ever in evidence round here?

G: Oh yes. He used to come down by rail and then get off at Chichester and come down on the road, and he'd stop here, there and everywhere, picking holes in the men's work and that.

DB: Did you ever meet him?

G: No, but I must admit that I've seen him. He used to come down to Selsey.

DB: Was he highly thought of?

G: Oh well, of course, he was in charge!

DB: Used people to respect him – was he feared?

G: Oh no, no. The only thing was, he had the money: he backed it!

Some might say that Mr. Green was eulogising a little – that the reality was not as attractive or as agreeable. But had his enthusiastic support for the line been shared by everybody, one wonders if the writer would still need to be describing the line in the past tense.

Appendix Three

The Women's Institute Play

The East Manhood Women's Institute plays a prominent part in the life of the local community. In 1980 the Women's Institute performed, for the entertainment of other Women's Institute groups in the locality, a play called *The train they called a tram*, concerned with the tramway and some of its stories, apocryphal and real. Here are some extracts from that play – the first piece of Selsey Tram-based entertainment since the *Sidlesham Snail Song*!

Enter Mary and Betty – two weary walkers.

Mary: Where are we?

Betty: This is Sidlesham, I think. Yes it must be the old railway. This book calls it the Hundred of Manhood and Selsey Tramway.

Mary: Why Manhood? More discrimination against women?

Betty: No, don't be silly Mary. Manhood is a corruption of Manewode from the Saxon which means Mainwood. When William the Conk came, all this peninsula was still mostly forest.

Mary: All right, Manhood means Mainwood. But why tram and/or train, and where is it now?

Betty: It ran from 1897 till 1935 and first was pulled by a steam engine and then later by a motor car on flanged wheels.

Mary: Did your Aunt tell you any stories about the train? I suppose she used it herself?

Betty: Yes, she didn't have a car. It was quite cheap, you know. Something like 1s. 2d. return to Chichester or 7½d. single. There were eight stops and three halts along the line. My Aunt told me that the engine driver would wait for someone who was late. On one occasion a child he knew asked him to wait while his father finished shaving.

Mary: Did he?

Betty: Oh, yes. Another time the train just stopped between stations and waited and waited, until one of the passengers asked what was wrong. He was told the fireman had dropped his tobacco pouch and had gone back to look for it! My Aunt said that the bridge over the canal at Hunston opened for some barges and got stuck for two days so the train couldn't pass.

Mary: Was there a lot of traffic on the line?

126

Betty: Oh, yes, especially in the summer when they were packed in like sardines. And they used to take goods – hay, lobsters, crabs and the then famous mouse traps. My Aunt told me that a young man she knew used to load hay for the Front during World War One at Chalder Farm, and when he went to the Front himself and looked after the horses, he found the hay he was unloading there was marked 'Chalder Farm'.

Mary: Look, the tide is coming in. Where does it come in?

Betty: Look at the gap between the single banks. I forgot about the flood in 1910. There was a terrific storm and a tidal surge and the sea broke in again and flooded right back through the fields and the line was under water. They had to raise it on an embankment because after that it flooded at every high tide.

This scene ends with the choir entering and singing the *Sidlesham Train* (*Sidlesham Snail?*) and Mary and Betty falling asleep, taking a nap after a well-earned lunch. Their dreamworld takes them back to Sidlesham station between 1905 and 1910.

Mrs. Carter: Hullo, Mrs. Hodges, are you going to market this morning? It looks like keeping fine for the cattle market.

Mrs. Hodges: Yes, Mrs. Carter, it does. I put my blankets to soak last night in the dolly tub, and this morning John helped me to put them over the clothes line and put the prop under them before setting off with his elevenses to take the heifers to market. He had the cattle up in long meadow last night, resting, before the driving them over to Donnington ridge so they won't be too tuckered by the time they get to market.

Mrs. Carter: Yes, at least the beasts don't fall into the canal now that the Council have put up strong rails either side of the road. (Enter Mrs. Brown)

Mrs. Brown: It's a pity old farmer Bailey don't fence off his piggery, then he wouldn't lose any pigs on the railway. Did you hear about the accident last week? Well, one of his sows got on the line, and my Bert was driving the train, and came round corner straight into it. You never heard such a squealing but the engine killed it stone dead. Well, Bert and Jack, the guard, didn't know what to do with it, so puts it in wagon with coal. Old farmer didn't seem to miss her so they cuts her up, and we had a fine roast on Sunday. I could let you both have a joint only mum's the word.

Mrs. Hodges: That would be very neighbourly of you, and save me paying a visit to the pork butcher in East Street, when I get to Chichester.

Mrs. Carter: Much obliged, Mrs. Brown. Did either of you know the other driver Jim Johnson [*sic*] and his fireman Fred Belcher?

Mrs. Brown: No, what happened to them? Did the engine go off line again Mrs. Carter?

Mrs. Carter: No, nothing like that. It was that party of weekenders from London. They wanted the train to hurry up so they could catch London train at Chichester. One of them tipped Fred Belcher, fireman, half a crown, and driver, Jim Johnson saw it. Well, somehow he couldn't get steam up, and then the brakes jammed so they were late at Stockbridge, and all the gents were fuming. The one who'd paid the tip came along to driver Jim and didn't he complain! Well, Jim took off his hat cap and said in that slow way of his, 'Seems to me, Sir, you oiled the wrong end of the train!' A real case of Sussex won't be druv![1]

Mrs. Hodges: That's a good yarn ... I must tell my husband about that! Ah, here comes the train ... we'd better get on the platform.

It is interesting to compare Mrs. Carter's version of this story the play with the version given by Mr. Green in Appendix Two.

The action now moves to Hunston station, the platform occupied by Mrs. Earwicker and Mrs. Brown and the following snatch of conversation which calls to mind a few more of the tramway's peculiarities:

Enter Mrs. Horner.

All: Morning.

Mrs. Horner: I thought I might have missed the tram, luckily it's late as usual – the children wanted to come but they wanted to ride in the truck, and they get so dirty when they do. I told them they could ride in the truck when they came home, but that wasn't good enough for them. So I gave them each a penny to buy sweets with, and left them under their Gran's eye.

Mrs. Earwicker: We could have asked him [the driver, presumably] to wait for you.

Mrs. Brown: He probably wouldn't have had enough steam. The last time we went to Chichester he tried to whistle at Stockbridge, and could only make a noise like ... (raspberry).

Train sound

Mrs. Earwicker: There's the train.

Mrs. Brown: Drat that man. He's passed the platform again.

It must be emphasised that this is only part of the play, but there is enough material in the extracts above to be able to recapture and convey to the audience of the Eighties, a little of the flavour of the tramway and its extraordinary differences from lines of the present age.

1. The reference to 'Sussex won't be druv' refers to a poem by W. Victor Cook. In many ways the tramway operation typifies this attitude:

Some folks as come to Sussex   But them as come to Sussex
They rackons as they knows   They mustn't push and shove
A darn sight better what to do   For Sussex will be Sussex
Than silly folks like me and you   And Sussex won't be druv.
Could possibly suppose.

Appendix Four

Tracing Old Railways

Those who followed the tramway route described in Chapter Eleven will recall the complete obliteration of evidence of a former rail route between Selsey Bridge and Selsey Town stations because of new housing. The shift of emphasis from rail to road transport and the great changes that have consequently been wrought in the English landscape since the last war, mean that there are hundreds more miles of former railway track which have been swallowed up into urban and other development and many people may be quite ignorant that locomotives once ran over the very ground on which their house now stands.

How does one go about looking for evidence of, and tracing, an old railway in one's neighbourhood? Most modern maps, even the largest-scale ones, cannot be relied upon to provide this information. Although the map reader will occasionally see a dotted line on the map carrying the words 'Disused Railway' or 'Course of old railway', these tend to be shown only where there is still some evidence of the railway's course in the landscape, for instance, a cutting, embankment or footpath.

The best sources of information in the first instance are old maps of the district. The heyday of the railways was in the first quarter of this century: it was only in the 1930s that the first signs of a break-up of this huge empire began to appear. It is not difficult to obtain Ordnance Survey maps printed in the immediate post-Great War years. If your secondhand bookshop does not oblige, Mr. Archer of The Pentre, Kerry, Newtown, Powys has a wide stock available. A splendid publication in 1991, the *Ordnance Survey Atlas of Victorian and Edwardian Britain*, has maps covering the entire island at the turn of the century. This may work out more cheaply than buying a large stock of old maps.

Having traced the existence of the railway and identified the starting point, terminus and intermediate stations, the real detective work begins. The growth of the Railway Ramblers has helped to increase dramatically the amount of old railway which has become public footpath, but, for the keen explorer, the real satisfaction lies in using existing landmarks such as roads, embankments and drawing imaginary lines between them to work out where a railway line, now totally obliterated, once went. Sometimes there is remarkably fine evidence of an old line, for instance the remains of a viaduct or the boarded up mouth of a tunnel.

The tracing process will be a frustrating one. Often the land will be private and access will be impossible: in that case there will be nothing for it but to continue to the next landmark and take up the line from there. Permission must always be sought to walk on private land and it should go without saying that walkers should never remove any railway evidence, such as brickwork or other lineside paraphernalia, for their own use. As well as being conduct amounting to theft, to hack away at brickwork could weaken the structure of which it is part.

To trace the line is one piece of detective work, and the next piece is to find out more about it. There are some old lines whose fame is almost legendary, the Somerset & Dorset Railway being one obvious example, but many branch lines will be far less well documented. The most obvious source of reference is the public library situated in the town or towns which are on the line in question; the library will contain a section devoted to local topography and a railway/transport section. The topographical books will not contain as much factual information as the specifically railway books, but may well contain anecdotes and other titbits surrounding the line and its users. If the line or part of it is a public footpath, look out also for footpath guides and details of local walks in the local information centre. If your line is covered, further background information may be available in these guides. If you wish to take some material away with you, you can of course, subject to copyright regulations, photo-copy material you find, or head for the town's booksellers and specifically their transport and local books section. Secondhand bookshops may even contain guides which mention the railway as still in existence. Owners of such shops may well have their own personal memories of the line or may be able to put you in touch with local residents who either travelled regularly or were in employment on the line. Even in today's fast moving world, there is a strong community spirit in many small towns. Of value too will be the town's museum, although the more important the line was to the town it served, the more likely it is that the museum will contain such things as old tickets, timetables and even station nameboards. The most valuable set of written memorabilia will be contained in the public record office usually situated in the county town for the county through which your line passes. There you will find old newspapers, correspondence, plans, pictures and perhaps even tape recordings chronicling the line. If you wish to use the facilities offered here, you must be prepared to fill in a form and supply proof of identity. You may also need to have a pencil with you, as ink may not be allowed.

The hardest things to come by are photographs and postcards. Railway postcards can fetch up to £40 or even more. If you see a photograph in a book which appeals to you, you may wish to write to the publisher to ascertain the source of the photo-graph. Many secondhand bookshops sell postcards or collections of them; a growth industry appears to be postcard sales, where collectors mingle in large halls, usually on Saturdays and Sundays, building up their albums. Many stallholders will stock a large selection of local cards, but beware: prices can be steep even for photographed reproductions. The Public Record Office may contain newspapers with photographs which could be copied, although the procedure for copying is a cumbersome and time-consuming one.

The result of your deliberations should be an impressive dossier of a way of life that has now gone for ever. It may well be that at that stage you will, like the writer, feel the urge to write your own history of the line to pass on to successive generations, none of whom will have any notion or memories of country railway travel.

Bibliography

Griffith, E., *The Hundred of Manhood and Selsey Tramway* (Herald Press, 1968)

Heron-Allen, E., 'Selseyana, 1906-37' (a collection of newspaper cuttings relating to Selsey housed in the West Sussex Record Office)

Kenward, J., *The Manewood Line* (1935)

Mee, F., *History of Selsey* (Phillimore, 1988)

Mitchell, V. and Smith, K., *Branch Line to Selsey* (Middleton Press, 1983)

'*Morous* and friends', *Model Railway Journal* Vol. 12 (1987)

Oppitz, L., *Sussex Railways Remembered* (Countryside Books, 1987)

Price, B., *Chichester, the Valiant Years* (Phillimore, 1978)

Railway Magazine   Vol. 2 Whitechurch, V. L. (1898)

                              Vol. 39 Whitechurch, V. L. (1916)

                              Vol. 76 Rush, R. W. and Nicol, H. (1935)

St John-Thomas, D., *The Country Railway* (Penguin Books, 1979)

Scott-Morgan, J., *The Colonel Stephens Railways* (David and Charles, 1978)

General archive material found in the West Sussex Record Office and Chichester District Museum including newspaper cuttings, letters and tapes from 1897 to the present.

The 1934 report by Southern Railway on the feasibility of adopting the Selsey Tramway.

Index

133

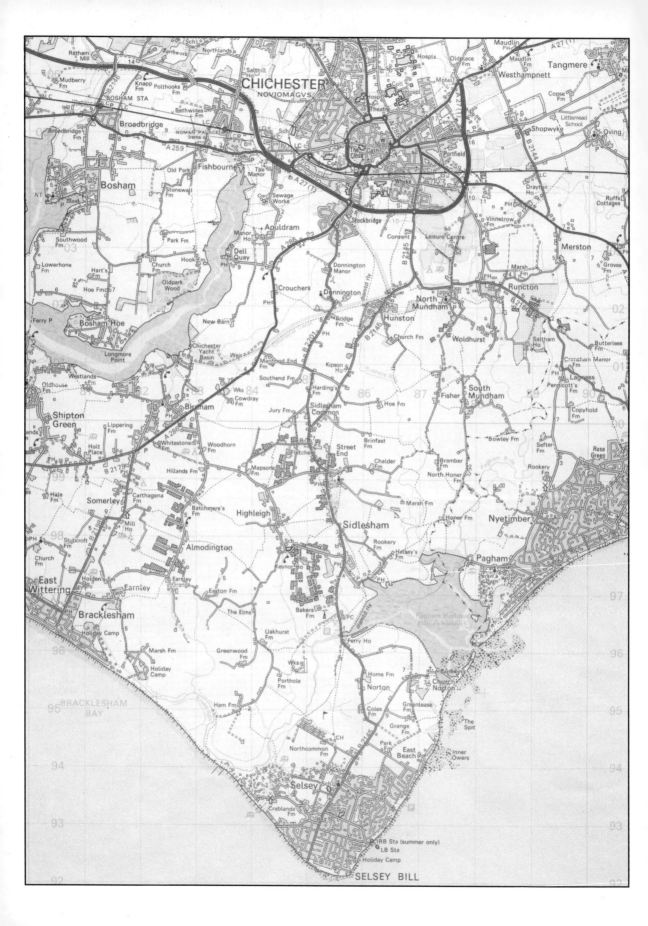